LOOKING TOWARD THE COUNCIL

ABOUT THE BOOK

The establishment of a Secretariat for Christian Unity in conjunction with the preparations for the Second Vatican Council indicates that the ultimate goal of the Council is the unification of all Christendom. No matter how remote such a goal may seem all valid efforts for attaining it must be applauded. Because of the world-wide and trans-confessional interest in the work of the Council, the present book draws upon Orthodox and Protestant viewpoints as well as Catholic. And though the emphasis in LOOKING TOWARD THE COUNCIL is on American expectations, there are also contributions by such distinguished continental theologians as Yves Congar, M. D. Chenu, and Hans Küng. This is the only book in English which brings together Catholics and non-Catholics, Americans and Europeans, clergy and laity in a discussion of the work of the forthcoming general Council.

QUAESTIONES DISPUTATAE

LOOKING
TOWARD THE COUNCIL

AN INQUIRY AMONG CHRISTIANS

EDITED BY

JOSEPH E. CUNNEEN

[from Cross Currents]

HERDER AND HERDER

1962

HERDER AND HERDER NEW YORK

232 Madison Avenue, New York 16, N. Y.

The chapters of this book originally appeared in "Cross Currents," published by Cross Currents Corporation, West Nyack, N. Y. The Publishers are very grateful to Cross Currents Corporation for permission to publish this book.

Nihil obstat: Austin B. Vaughan, S.T.D.
Censor Librorum
Imprimatur: ✠ Francis Cardinal Spellman
Archbishop of New York
August 23, 1962

The nihil obstat and imprimatur are official declarations that a book or pamphlet is free of doctrinal or moral error. No implication is contained therein that those who have granted the nihil obstat and imprimatur agree with the contents, opinions or statements expressed.

Library of Congress Catalog Card Number: 62-19562
Made and printed in the United States of America

CONTENTS

Introduction

The Second Vatican Council is an event which merits a rather special response in this series. In fact, from one point of view the Council can be seen as a climax to various stirrings within the Catholic community to give greater reality—and possibly institutional status—to the idea of a public opinion in the Church. This book is offered as a gesture of gratitude and loyalty; it is intended as an example of, and a contribution to, that state of mind in which all Catholics may more responsibly play their parts in this new age of the Council.

The reader will find only natural that in this work of preparation a substantial contribution should be expected from our Christian friends who are not Roman Catholics. We cannot help but assume that all can profit from the questions and reflections of those who share a common Baptism and whom the Pope wished would associate themselves in the preparation of the Council.[1] Although the use of the term "ecumenical" in announcing the Council led to confusion at the outset, and it soon became clear that this was to be a Council essentially of the Roman Catholic Church, it is equally important to remember that the Council was, from the beginning, conceived in the context of reconciliation. The first condition of this reconciliation was that the Church undertake a self-examination, with a view to purification and renewal. The establishment of a Secretariat for Christian Unity, the increased and sympathetic interest in the work of the World Council of Churches, and various declarations of such official spokesmen as Cardinal Bea—all make it clear that if the Council is primarily a matter of Catholics taking stock of their own situation, it is by way of a return to the common source of Christianity, and hence by itself constitutes a major step towards reunion.

If, then, the Council is an event which should not leave any Christian indifferent, this does not mean that it is unimportant for others. Although they are not represented in this issue, it is to be hoped that the voices of Jews, Moslems, indeed all who believe in God and non-believers as well, may yet be heard from after the event, sharpening our realization of this moment of time in whose redemption we must all cooperate.

---

1 Cf. the pontifical allocution of Nov. 14, 1960, *La Documentation catholique*, Dec. 4, 1960, p. 1484.

It is impossible to provide a balanced account of the various stages of response to Pope John's initiative. In the beginning there appeared to be considerable enthusiasm, often accompanied by strange misconceptions and naive utopianism. This may have had its dangers, but it created a more useful atmosphere for constructive work than the considerable skepticism that succeeded it. Whatever the real facts, the popular image received was one of fences quickly being erected to limit the horizon, as if the Pope needed a course in prudence from the members of the Holy Office. The sense of a return to routine, a feeling that the changeless character of doctrine was being made an excuse for the evasion of a genuine and loyal desire for self-reform, has affected both Catholics and those Christians who have followed with greatest sympathy the various movements of biblical, liturgical and theological renewal in the Church. This perhaps overhasty sense of disappointment has even affected the preparation of this issue.

The total picture of the Christian world on the eve of the Council must take into consideration the unwillingness of some responsible Protestant spokesmen—by no means "anti-Catholic"—to contribute to our symposium, feeling that the Council could have a profound effect only on the Catholic Church, since there was no genuine meeting of minds with representatives of other churches. Perhaps even more significant, there was also considerable reluctance on the part of many Catholics, both priests and laymen, who are actively involved in various movements of the contemporary apostolate. Although they do not confuse the Council with the House of Representatives, they obviously believe that their experience provides them with a relevant word to be added to the total response made to the Pope's appeal. The belief that it is useless for them to say what is on their mind, or that frankness will be immediately misread as irreverence or a bid for publicity, is in itself part of the condition which should give a sense of urgency to the work of the Council.

This book, then, was created partly to fill a lacuna in the presentation of the suggestions and criticism of the Christian world. Although conditions undoubtedly vary from place to place, and there are often contradictory indications from the same source, one can only report the over-all sense that too little has been done, at least within the American Catholic community, to alert the faithful to the meaning and importance of this coming event in the life of the Church. Some bishops, it is true, have issued exemplary pastoral letters on the Council, instituted diocesan committees on Christian unity, or provided a more regular channel for the expression of lay opinion. For whatever reason, however, on the local level, and as mirrored in the popular Catholic press, there has been more energy displayed in the concern for federal

8

aid for parochial schools than in the preparation of the faithful for the Council.

This book, presented as a contribution to that preparation, had its origin in a questionnaire on the Council, "An Inquiry among Christians," distributed by the editors of *Esprit*, the international monthly founded by Emmanuel Mounier; the results were published in a special issue, December 1961. Much of this enquiry, plus additional articles by American contributors, were published in *Cross Currents*, Spring 1962. It was also found appropriate to add, as postscripts to the symposium, although not written specifically for it, a discussion by Asian and African laymen, a recent address by Cardinal Bea, and a brief article by Hans Kueng.

Since the contributors were left completely free in their responses, and did not know the contents of the other articles that were submitted, there are inevitable repetitions as well as some interesting contrasts of attitude which we have no intention of resolving. It is not our business to provide a commentary or a synthesis; we can only plead that these testimonies be taken seriously, as they have been offered, in no partisan spirit, but in humility and hope.

JOSEPH E. CUNNEEN

M. D. Chenu

The Churches Conciliar Life and the Sociology of Faith

Among the many studies stimulated by the preparation for the coming Council, one of the most suggestive is among those published in the remarkable collection *Le Concile et les Conciles* and written by M. A. Dupront, professor of modern history at the University of Paris.[1] Having been asked, as one of the series of speakers on the Church's conciliar life, to speak on the Council of Trent, M. Dupront confronts his subject as an historian, to be sure, but as an historian whose path converges with the theologian's. In the course of investigating Trent's significance, he was led to come to terms with those sociological dimensions with which, generally speaking, neither history nor theology comes to grips; and it is in fact, these same sociological factors which give to the historical phenomenon (even the sacred phenomenon) its real significance. For the sociological realities are, after all, as fundamental to the life of religion and the Church as they are to the realm of the profane.

We are not directly concerned in this essay with such sociological factors, factors which frequently are buried beneath the surface in the deliberations and even in the texts of the Councils; the more unconscious these sociological realities in the collective sensibility, the more powerful they are as determining factors. In fact the "Mediterranean character" of the participants, the majority role of the religious orders, the formulation of a *doctrina* by men of an academic cast of mind, the deliberative power of the theologians behind the prelates, a certain taste for the security of verbal definitions, the crystallization of the orthodox state of mind, the total inattention to the relevant socio-economic realities—realities which can and do transform both man's earthly condition as well as the behavior of the faithful—all of these sociological factors, despite their "secular" origin, enter into the conceptual and doctrinal

---

1 *Le Concile et les Conciles* (Paris, ed. du Cerf, 1960, xx, pp. 348). They are the texts of papers read at a colloquy held at Chèvetogne, Belgium.

Father M. D. Chenu, O.P., was formerly Dean of Studies of Saulchoir and is a distinguished historian of theology.

fabric of most theological formulations as well as most religious inspirations. Those familiar with M. Dupront's monograph have seen the unusual benefits to be derived from such a method.

Taking Dupront's analysis as a point of departure, I should here like to show, by reference to other Councils, how such approaches yield more than those factors which are ultimately accidental and non-essential to the understanding and expression of the faith proclaimed at these assemblages. Such analyses, on the contrary, reveal in this very faith a properly interior dimension which governs both its perceptions and its pronouncements. In every point of its elaboration, in its ecclesial support, in its final structure, the pronouncement of a Council, whether doctrinal or disciplinary, emerges out of a "communion" of thought, out of a social consciousness which is not the sum total of the efforts, the lights, the private fervors of the assembled individuals. The pronouncement is rather the result of a collective phenomenon having, according to the sociology of knowledge, both its own laws and its own unique norms—an essential and fruitful relativity. Just as the faith of an individual is structured and manifested in accordance with the laws of the individual psychology of intelligence, so in the same way the faith of a Council is elaborated, structured and formulated in terms of the sociology of the spirit. Even though it remains true that faith is, in a special way, within the believer, still, adherence to the Word of God and to the light of the Holy Spirit neither totally dissolves nor disqualifies those laws, methods, processes and problems which go to make up the natural operations of the intelligence. When God reveals himself to man, he doesn't do so in terms of the modes of his [God's] own understanding, but according to the modes of the human mind, including the humble operations of grammar and language. If this divine communication takes place within a community called the Church, it will, in the process of being humanized, likewise follow the laws, the operations of collective knowing which any sociologist can point out in any human society.

The scope of such a notion of faith, of faith in action in a Council, is easily determined. Certainly the believer, trusting in the permanence and development of the word of God within the Community of the Church, will refer to the active assistance of the Holy Spirit as final cause; the believer will, however, acknowledge that secondary causes, sociological as well as individual, are in fact the components of the Holy Spirit's action. The believer holds, furthermore, that the Holy Spirit's presence is not realized by some sort of mystical bypassing of these causalities, reducing them to the level of mere preliminaries, but rather by and in these very causalities, beginning with the language, the mental climates, the collective experience of the pastors, the technical analyses of the theologians, the imperceptible or sometimes impassioned give and take which occurs both during and after the deliberative sessions. One might almost speak of the humanity of the Holy Spirit within the Church He assists, in much the same way that there was a full humanity of Christ in the primitive Apostolic community. It is, on the modest level of assistance, the same law of incarnation. We must effectively resist the permanent temptation of a false idealism, which both in its vision of the Church and in its understanding of Christ, severs the human reality from the divine. (This is, in technical language, the "monophysite" error.) Otherwise faith becomes nothing more than the unattainable absolute of an interior light, finding its base in a pure obedience to the external pronouncements of a magisterium. The result is a decay of intelligence, a decay caused by a blockage of dogmatism and mysticism. The history of the Church's conciliar life as well as theological good sense rejects such integralism.

It is regrettable, then, that in the present perspective of the Council there is developing here and there a certain soothing and monotonously dithyrambic literature in which, under the pretense of extolling the work of the Holy Spirit, there is, sometimes deliberately, a juggling, a playing down of the human elements and the tensions whose interplay is a matter of normal development. It would be better to confront this play of tensions candidly from the point of view of a precise theology of faith. This tension, historically rooted in human diversities and in variegated group values, includes human limitations, faults, passions, dissensions, even rejections of one person by another. It is the task of faith to be educated and informed according to its own laws of truth, and not to close its eyes under the pretext of obeying the Holy Spirit. When M. Dupront, as a good historian, distinguishes the human causalities at work in the deliberations and decisions of the Council of Trent, he is not simply yielding to a curiosity which is useful to the scholar but inappropriate to the believer. This is good, sound theology (the theologians, as a matter of fact, have been engaging in fruitful dialogue with him); it is theology striving to come to a genuine understanding of that faith shared by the Fathers of the Council.[2]

It is up to us to do the same thing today in the course of our preparation for the second Vatican Council, and to do so in a spirit of healthy openness. As Congar, quoting Pascal, puts it: "What spoils it for us, says Pascal, in our efforts to compare what took place in the Church in earlier times with what is going on in the present, is that one usually thinks of St. Athanasius, St. Teresa and others as deities crowned with glory.... But when they were being persecuted, they were simply a man named

_____

[2] The *Fathers of the Council* participate in the deliberations of the assembly. By right, they are bishops or prelates who administer a diocese, as well as the superior general of the great orders. Titular bishops, who do not really have the responsibility of a diocese can, if invited by the pope, also participate. The preparatory commissions, besides certain fathers of the council, include *consultors* who have only an advisory voice. (Tr.)

Athanasius and a young woman named Teresa."[3] This necessary work of preparation is, to some extent, now going on, at the express invitation of the hierarchy, prelates and simple theologians, qualified, self-conscious priests and laymen, especially in the churches of Germany, Austria and Holland.[4]

The major task of the historian is to distinguish contexts without which the data and the texts would be nothing more than raw material, devoid of meaning. The chief work of the sociologist, similarly, is the analysis of those relationships which in any way condition events and decisions, not only from without but even in their internal dynamism. Thus, in its sociological density, faith organizes its perceptions and its statements only in terms of its commitment, which conditions it humanly and ecclesially in much the same way as—and maybe even more than —an individual's faith is conditioned by his birth and environment, his temperament, his culture, his problems and his experience.

As for the coming Council, the first thing to be noted is that there is a certain set of circumstances leading up to and surrounding the summoning of the Church to a Council, that there is, in short, a conciliar "conjuncture." The very calling of the Council was itself a surprise, the result of the spontaneous initiative of John XXIII (in January 1959), coming as it did without any official consultation or organized deliberations. It was even more surprising from the point of view of the many Christian circles which tended to feel that the era of Councils had come to a close. The weight of the Vatican Council of 1870, which had determined the role of the Sovereign Pontiff without getting around to examining the other organs of the Church, in fact led to a certain depreciation of them. Some were led to think that, especially in a world more and more dominated by great organizations, a concentration of definitions, decisions, and even of government by the Roman Curia, would seem to be a normal and effective development. But now it is the Church's turn to speak in its universal assembly, whose role it is to bring together the experiences, the concerns, the problems, and the hopes of each and all of us, since all the bishops (about 2600 of them) in company with and surrounding the Bishop of Rome, are going to have to raise their voices, freely and firmly, as authentic members of the magisterium and government of the Church.

It is not only a question of "continuing" the interrupted Council of

---

3 The text of Pascal, *Pensées*, fr 866, is cited by Fr. Congar (*Le Concile et les conciles*, p. 319), who shows that the very human and fully historical character of the councils is not a matter of a few peripheral occurrences, but is linked to their very structure, and that this is for the purpose of a full understanding of the effective action of God.

4 Among other examples, we may cite the frank and vigorous statements of Cardinal Koenig of Vienna, of Archbishop Jaeger of Paderborn, of Dr. O. Roegele, director of RHEINISCHER MERKUR (1961), the collection of articles in WORT UND WAHRHEIT (1961), articles in REVUE NOUVELLE, etc.

1870 and of completing its chapter on the powers of the pope by a second chapter on the status of the bishops. It is also a question of giving consciousness and presence, in the person of its bishop, to each local church, which in a certain manner actualizes the universality of the institution. The institutional and spiritual coherence of the Church is established not only by means of a vertical relationship between the local cells and the supreme pontiff, but established simultaneously, and no less necessarily, through the horizontal relationships of these cells to each other within the unified body. The Council is, consequently, a normal organism, through which this body breathes and lives. The congregations which, like so many ministers, assist the pope (and in a fair number of regions the patriarch of the West rather than the pope as such) cannot be substituted for the organism which is the Council. "The Councils are the exact opposite of a central organism linked to a single power; they are the 'total church,' that is, all of the local churches spread across the earth, assembled for the purpose of experiencing and deliberating together."[5] The fact that conciliarism, the theory which would subordinate the pope to the Council, is no longer a real threat emphasizes the truth of the Council as an institution within which the areas of supreme power can be coordinated.

At the Council of Trent there was already evidence of this tension between the Pontifical Curia and conciliar initiative. The pope, either on his own or through his legates, had repeatedly supported and guaranteed the assembly's initiative in the face of certain obstacles. It is no secret that today the convocation of John XXIII has encountered some respectful opposition; without going into the many significant episodes, we can, nevertheless, see that during this pre-Council period, given over to the work of the more than 700 experts on the dozen commissions and secretariats, the principle has been affirmed that these commissions constitute an organism institutionally different from and independent of the Roman Curia.

One must, consequently, take seriously the hierarchy's renewed appeal for a collective awakening of the faithful in their local churches. "It is indeed up to you," they are constantly being told, to shake off the inertia which is sapping faith. Such an awakening is coming about, however slowly; it is an awakening of the active consciousness of the Community, an awakening to the very fact of its essential, societal organisms. This phenomenon is, moreover, a peculiarly religious one; despite certain similarities, it is of quite a different order than the manifestation of democratic sentiments in the political sphere. Sociologists, regardless of their personal allegiances, note this as one of the most intense expressions of religion to be found in Christianity. Another such example is to be found in the Moslem *Umma*, whose institutional trappings, however, are quite different from the Christian hierarchy. And yet the *Umma*, in

---

[5] Cf. O. Rousseau, *Le Concile et les conciles*, pp. xvi-xviii.

its own way and on its own terms, has a remarkable value and a cogency, primarily in terms of religious intensity but also from the point of view of its secular consequences. In the Church this communal consciousness —which raises many psychological and institutional problems—has been tending to reverse that individualistic spirituality which has been raging for several centuries. This sense of community, furthermore, is thrusting upon the Christian that extraordinary sensibility which in our time is catching up individuals, groups, nations, economies, even whole masses into a new civilization. We have still to see what this new solidarity, once fully realized, will lead to—that solidarity which is at work on all sides and which in itself provides a good reason to consider the convocation of the Council in terms other than those of merely confessional concerns.

The surest indication of the scope of the coming council is the fact that it rather quickly went beyond what seemed initially to have been its clear purpose. Some observers concluded from Pope John's initial statements that the good envisaged was the re-unification of the Church after the long separation resulting from the Eastern schism and the Protestant reformation. Although this goal in no sense disappeared, it found itself absorbed into a larger perspective in which the hope for a fraternal reconciliation was now seen as one of the fruits of a renewal which would affect the internal operations and structures of the Church itself, making it more attractive and placing it in a position of open dialogue. As the leading force in this dialogue, the Secretariat for Christian unity, while retaining its star role—of which some disapprove—is really only one manifestation, in a particular area, of a general movement of the ecclesial body, a movement which indicates the growing recognition of the needs and problems involved in encountering humanity as a whole. The work of unity is only the condition and the exercise of the Church's "mission" in and to the world.

The maturity of this many-sided movement gives to the coming Council certain features which, in terms both of its hopes and its resources, distinguish it in advance from many other councils, where the call to assemble went out as a result of some heresy, during a hard and restrictive crisis when some truth in the deposit of faith was being threatened. Such a defense reaction was necessary, but it led to that type of crystallization, spoken of by M. Dupront, which operated to the detriment of the fullness and harmony of doctrine. Christians today are, of course, confronted by a world in which atheism has tragically supplanted heresy; at least within itself, by diverse theological options or pastoral concerns, the Church does not see the common riches of its faith questioned, as it unhappily experienced in the struggles with Luther and Calvin in the sixteenth century, and even as in the early centuries of its existence it was afflicted by doctrinal disturbances concerning the person of Christ. It follows, therefore, that in the present circumstances, neither general opinion, nor the theologians, nor the pope himself, are orienting the coming assembly toward theoretical discussions and definitions, interspersed with a few anathemas. We see here, no doubt, the reflection of the personal qualities of Pope John's brand of leadership, in which an emphasis upon the "pastoral" rather than the doctrinal has frequently been noted; this is certainly not the result of any lukewarm attitude towards the truth; it represents rather an inclination to work out this truth in the concrete order. This personal tendency finds support and agreement among the majority of theologians and prelates. Most of them in fact feel that, at the present moment, the love of truth is more efficacious, more "true," in the intrepid witness of dialogue than in the protectionism of interdicts and defensive bulwarks.

Nor does the Council envisage a "general reform," in the technical sense of the word. All during the early middle ages fervent pastors, the mighty, the humble, and even political sovereigns, were constantly clamoring for a reformation *in capite et in membris*. The Council of Trent was the modern type of this concern and this effort, and in the laborious post-history of this Council the pontiffs have extended its decisions even into difficult areas of Catholicism. But the polarization of this momentous spiritual conflict as a result of an obsession with a counter-reformation led to diminished perspectives at the very moment when, through the scientific exploration of the world—and soon of man—western humanity was entering, by means of socio-economic transformations, into "modern times." The Council Fathers, while committed to certain necessary reforms, had no presentiment of that evolution of minds and institutions which had, in fact, already begun. If we were to seek the first signs of the Christian exile, his alienation from his world, we would have to go back to that point, well before the nineteenth century.

Even by the time of the Fourth Lateran Council, at the high point of the middle ages, the Church found itself facing analogous pressures for reform. It was this very urgency which imposed limitations on its program and which gave a certain cast to its decisions. The renewed awareness of spiritual and apostolic needs (a recognition forged amidst hardships and anarchy, in the sub-stratum of existing institutions) was hardly even echoed in the assembly halls of the Council. The 412 bishops and 800 abbots and priors who made up the Fourth Lateran Council remained unconsciously linked to a feudal regime which had provided them with material and religious security; they remained likewise insensitive to the conditions of a newly emancipated generation. Thus we can see the truth of the statement that spiritual ends are hardly to be realized outside of a human communion. It was Francis of Assisi and Dominic the preacher who, operating as they were outside of the structures of their times, discerned and effected the kind of break needed for a return to the Gospels. It was the genius of Innocent III, himself a great potentate, that sheltered and protected their initiative, and, flying in the face of the conservative condemnations of the Council, guaranteed Francis and Dominic both personal and institutional freedom. And it was through such means that the Council's decrees achieved their force-fulness and truthfulness.

Through such references to the past we are able to recognize the problems which, at certain moments of history, confront the body of Christians. It is no longer a problem involving this or that reform or refutation; it is rather a question of existence itself. Immersed in a world which they have evangelized—or at least sacralized and civilized—Christians are taking stock and coming to realize that this world, in its social trappings, its culture, its spirit, is in the process of slipping into the past, and that unforeseen values are emerging out of the transformations now taking place. This is all to the benefit of a new human condition, since man's developing nature is one which is infinitely malleable and creative. Evolution, rebirth, revolution, period, epoch, era—these are ambiguous categories utilized by historians to describe and measure the phenomenon, but they have the advantage of suggesting the collective character of those mutations which are leading the individual person to the profoundest depths of his own freedom.

This freedom is at once furthered and restricted by the determining conditions arising out of the union of matter and spirit. The faith of the believer may, in its temporal situation and its psychological reflexes, be exposed to these irresistible pressures which, depending on the occasion, can be either beneficent or threatening. Faith, however, must not in itself be disconcerted by human change; the word of God, in the passage of time and for a people on the move, is, through its very transcendence, fit to become incarnate in the variants of civilizations as well as in the ages of individuals, in the different sectors of society or geographical areas, in classes as well as in nations.

It remains true that, healthily and happily involved in one or another sociological situation, faith does not always experience the relativity of its temporal conditions, and because of this obstacle to thought and expression finds itself "expatriated" in new human continents. This kind of uprooting, this time lag, has occurred several times in history, and even if faith's immutable truth is ultimately guaranteed against contamination, the efficacy of its incarnation is none the less reduced and compromised. Feudal Christendom maintained an attitude of bitter defiance toward the newly flowering towns and the new freedom of young university scholars, intoxicated by the new spirit of Aristotelian-Arabic science. Christendom during the *Quattrocento*, in spite of its complacent attitude toward the revival of interest in the arts and letters, did not really come to terms with the thrust for autonomy in the realm of knowledge and politics. Nineteenth-century Christendom, in the heyday of bourgeois liberalism, experienced what was called the "conflict between religion and the modern world"—as if the "religion" in question was abstract deism rather than evangelical Christianity. In such historical circumstances as these the "reformism" of the Councils was not proportionate to the problems posed.

Today we are faced with changes which affect every area of human reality from the economic to the spiritual. These changes include technological progress, socialization, demography, the structure of politics, decolonization, the secularization of the world's problems, scientific rationalism, the tendency to reduce human relationships to a kind of behavioristic rationalism, man's increasing control over nature and the growth of ideologies and myths. Faced with such radical transformations, the western Christian in particular is at first disconcerted, if only by the geographic dimension of the problem of his presence in the world. His anxiety springs largely from the difficulty he faces in attempting to distinguish and disentangle from within the unquestionable values of the Western tradition, of "Christian civilization," the permanent and necessary expression of God's word from those things which are contingent and non-essential. The latter are free to be acted upon by the experience and knowledge of new conditions which are attendant upon a humanity itself in the process of evolving. The anguish of the contemporary Christian conscience is incontestable—and certain kinds of anguish, we must remember, are healthy—when we see that most of the components of this new civilization are emptying it of any sacral quality, and even, at least at this moment, seem to tend toward atheism.[6] The attempt to take stock of our situation, even if somewhat feverish, is none the less active, both in its sense of hope and in its diagnostic views of a Christianity which, along with the purity of the Gospel, is re-discovering its own catholicity. This catholicity is, in the first instance, geographic—a dimension of the Church which has, of course, been periodically affirmed in its missionary activity, but from now on will be forced to achieve a truly indigenous presence among newly awakened masses. This re-discovered sense of catholicity has, furthermore, a social dimension which will be ultimately indigenous to the working classes and aware of the Christian resources available within a technological civilization, which is, to a large extent, still looked upon with fear. This catholicity we are discussing is, finally, cultural in scope. Without giving up any of the acquisitions of our western tradition, this new sense of catholicity will no longer force either faith or the expression of that faith into the merely temporal, localized confines of a fixed, static humanism—beginning with the grammatical categories of a dead language. For more than a thousand years now the Councils have been "Latin," in personnel, in expression, in mentality and in the kinds of problems posed. Today we simply must go beyond the age of Constantine. This is being said on all sides, with some bitterness, since the

6 Cf. "Is the modern world atheist," an interview with Fr. Chenu and Friedrich Heer, *Cross Currents*, Winter 1961. (Tr.)

Constantinian era is seen as an age during which renewals and reforms, both good and bad, were after all nothing more than so many episodes in a univocal history. The world exists for us, after all, at this point in time and henceforth into the future, and any problem which is not posed in terms of this world of ours is a problem badly posed and, consequently, a problem admitting of no solution. The coming Council will have to pose the problem of the Church, the problem of faith in terms of *our* world, the admirable and frightful world of 1962.

The importance of reforms and renewals must not, of course, be either slighted or ignored—the liturgical reform, the rebirth of truly Christian communities, the renewal of apostolic methods, the restoration of the episcopal function—all these items are on the agenda for the coming Council. These major tasks, however, will receive their illumination and their energy only by hearkening to a new world, a world which waits expectantly.

The bishops, in reaffirming their "collegiality," their solidarity in working together, are actually doing nothing more than manifesting an institutional awareness of the catholicity of the apostolic Church.

We can see multiplying on all sides the signs and expressions of this awareness of which we have been speaking. They were, at first, little more than foreshadowings, and the appeals by the prophets were, on the whole, but poorly understood. Under the pressure of events, however, certain spiritual and apostolic experiences have accrued, experiences which have proven to be veritable laboratories for the Gospel in the world. The hierarchy has now taken charge of these experiences, occasionally disputing and blurring them in the process, and is preparing to record them, to confront them from Paris to Bandung, from India to Madagascar, and to evaluate and analyze the basic, underlying needs. Was it not, after all, one of the high prelates of the defunct Holy Roman Empire who adopted, by way of diagnosing our present situation, the slogan about the end of the Constantinian Era.[7] We already have, do we not, certain rather remarkable decisions of Popes Pius XI and XII, together with certain of their commentaries on texts of their predecessors, and these decisions and commentaries were indeed ahead of the day-to-day conduct of their regimes.

It is not so much that Christendom is dying as that it is transmitting its heritage into other hands in response to pressures which it will ulti- mately come to recognize as providential.

The Church is disentangling itself from a Christendom whose successes and honors have proven to be no guarantee against inertia or loss of social position. It is by becoming a missionary Church whose mission is to a new kind of world that the Church is re-discovering itself. The Church is re-discovering itself through its involvement in a mission to the world, by getting outside of itself, outside of its comfortable secur-

---

7 Archbishop Jaeger of Paderborn, in an article in ECHO DER ZEIT, Jan. 31, 1960.

ity. And this is its nature, its primary nature. It is the Church's nature as stated at the 1959 general assembly of the French hierarchy, to address itself first of all to "those who are apart [*loin*]." Those who are apart are clearly the peoples who have attained an economic and political existence which is as much beyond cultural and apostolic colonialism as it is beyond economic colonialism. The leaders of these peoples are already keeping an eye on the preparations for this Council, and they will perhaps have both the occasion and the means for getting around certain stages which the ancients of the West have neither the freedom nor the understanding to bypass.

Those who are apart are, furthermore, the ones who, within traditional Christendom itself, inhabit the "mission territories" which the secular, profane world will henceforth be constructing through science, technology, increased leisure, human relations, the international life, the rights of man, the grand aspirations of humanity. In the words of Congar, "The coming Council is going to have to be a Council in which the Church, by questioning itself in terms of the questions of our time, will be able to define itself in an open and generous manner, not so much in and for itself as in its relationship to the world and in the relationship which the Others have with her."[8]

Thus the *historicity* of the faith is, in the Community, the test of faithfulness. Faith is a totally interior light, irreducibly personal and free, in each believer. Faith is given objectively, it is received through the hearing of a Word, a Word which the apostolic succession transmits and guarantees. In terms of the two poles, which cannot be coordinated without a certain tension, the dialectic is resolved in a Church in which person and community mutually interact—to the advantage and fullness of each, in a sacred history. For God speaks *today*; and that can come about only if his Church is present to the world.

Translated by JAMES J. GREENE

---

8 Y. M.-J. Congar, in the conclusion of the volume *Le Concile et les conciles*, p. 329; and "The Council, the Church, and the 'Others'," CROSS CURRENTS, Summer 1961.

Inquiry Among Christians

Catholics, Orthodox, Anglicans and Protestants were asked the following questions:

1. how do you look on the next Vatican Council? What importance do you attribute to it for the future of the Catholic Church? For the reconciliation of Christian Churches, and the progress of faith in the world?

2. what are, in your opinion, the principal themes which the Council should take up? Where are the points where a reform, or a renewal or innovation, seems particularly desirable to you?

3. in order that the Council be an essential stage on the way to the reunion of Churches, a great effort of purification and renewal is demanded of Catholicism. How do you conceive of this effort as regards the Catholic Church? As regards other churches? At what levels do you place the confrontation of faith with the world and with contemporary humanism? For you, what are the principal obstacles and lines of convergence?

Yves M. J. Congar

The Council in the Age of Dialogue

Several times I have heard it said, "The Council is coming twenty-five years too soon. Neither the work in progress in the revival of Biblical studies, nor the liturgical renewal, nor the ecumenical dialogue, nor recent pastoral studies have yet reached either its own dynamic development or its full audience. We would be in a better position in a quarter of a century...." All of this reminds me of what was said to me one day by Père de Vaux, director of *L' École Biblique* in Jerusalem. We were standing on a site in Palestine which was in the process of being excavated. "We are thieves!" he said. "Renan in his day, on behalf of the devil, prepared the very excavations we are improving upon today. In twenty-five years, they will be using methods which will make our own efforts look like bungling or the work of a common ditch-digger. Still, we must dig. In twenty-five years, they will explore in detail those things which our work today only permits us to guess at."

All of this may be applied analogously to the second Vatican Council; it will be at least a beginning. It will probably not give all the results desired by those who take part in the movements mentioned above —especially in the matter which has raised hopes highest: ecumenism, the dialogue with the Others. This would not disturb us if we had a total view of history, but we go on in time as if we were walking backwards: we see only the past, what we leave behind us. That is why the Council of 1962–63 for us will seem to be the last one. Actually, it will be only the twenty-first; there will be a twenty-second, and doubtless still others. To be truly wise, a man should include the future and its possibilities in his vision and appreciation. The Council will help greatly to form patience in us, not only in the sense of the practical attitude of the man who knows how to wait, but also as a quality of intelligence, an aspect of realism.

This has greater importance as we learn more and more to think his-

Father Yves Congar, O.P., is a major Catholic spokesman on ecumenism, the role of the layman, and the theology of the Church. His most recent book is LA TRADITION ET LES TRADITIONS *(Fayard).*

torically. It is certainly not necessary to view our predecessors as more naive than they were; but we ought to stop thinking of them as being gifted with exactly the same mental tools and endowments as ourselves. They had a most naive grasp of facts and of their proper meaning. History has become a dimension of our way of thinking and of our judgments. We place things and ourselves in a complete unfolding sequence. We are not content to accept things simply as they are in themselves; we consider them as under the glance of history and of the world. We know that we are judged by history and we anticipate that judgment by appraising the events with which we are involved as part of a continuous pattern. The present juncture asks for a certain response on our part, or for certain initiatives that would be in harmony with world change. We have a lively sense of the historical failure, the lost opportunity, the myopia with regard to events or the deafness to the appeals of the times. Some will doubtless be disappointed in the Council. They are hoping that it will be a complete answer to all that they consider to be in question. But it is unlikely that the Council will bring about all that. From what can be seen of the preparations—from the outside, of course—the Council promises to keep a middle course between, on the one hand, a simple traditional activity, limited to protect or promote a suitable form of ecclesiastical system; and on the other, what St. Bernard has already called, about 1150, *"quod tempus requirit,"* what the times demand. It will *begin* to give an answer to the requests of history, while looking forward to another part of the work to be done.

But to tell the truth, in proposing this view, I only mean that I don't *know,* that I am guessing. In the months to come, we will probably hear repeated the saying of Pius IX concerning the first Vatican Council: "A Council always goes through three phases. First, there is the phase of the Devil; then the phase of men; and finally the phase of God." Does the Devil know that he has lost his chance? Or is he saving himself for later? It does not seem that his intervention has yet been perceived. The two other protagonists remain. They represent great unknown elements.

As for men, it is not yet known what they will say, for the Council has not begun. It is true that eleven commissions and three secretariats have been functioning for a year, but they are *pontifical* commissions, organized by the Pope to *prepare* for the Council. It is true that the Holy Father has organized them in a very "conciliar" manner. For one thing, he has arranged these groups of preparatory workers in terms of the results of the examination of 2700 responses received from the bishops of the entire world, from the Roman Congregations, from Nuncios and universities; they were asked to speak freely on how they saw the overall problem, and what questions they wished to discuss. The extent of this step is more significant if one remembers that in preparing for the first Vatican Council, Pius IX secretly consulted 35 Latin bishops chosen by himself, then, several weeks later, 35 Oriental bishops. Another sign of the times is the fact that the commissions and secretariats have been made up in an extremely "catholic" fashion, which to some degree prefigures the conciliar assembly.

One factor remains. This is the coming together of all the bishops of the world. There is a particular dynamism, it could be said even a particular grace, in the meeting of men. One does not have to espouse the system of Durkheim to say that an assembly is something original; it develops something different from what may be expected from the list of individuals originally called together. When the bishops arrived for the first Vatican Council, they were given the statements of the projects prepared by theologians; they began by rejecting them, finding that they did not correspond with their wishes and that they were too scholastic in their form. Ultimately, it is true, many of the original statements were approved in their second versions and in the Council itself. It cannot be foreseen what the reaction of the bishops will be concerning the statements now being prepared by the pre-conciliar pontifical commissions; nor can one predict what will come from the reunion of bishops, what voices will rally others, or which events will, perhaps, determine developments that now are unforeseeable.

Then, there is the Holy Spirit. Each Council proclaims itself "legitimately assembled in the Holy Spirit," following the first apostolic synod at Jerusalem, which began its decree with the words: "It has seemed good to the Holy Spirit and to us." God—or, according to other valid points of view, one can say "Christ," or "The Holy Spirit"—is an active person in the Council; something like the situation in a Christian marriage, in which there are not only a man and a woman, but a third person, who concludes the marriage contract at the same time as they do and makes their contract a sacrament. We profess to believe in the Holy Spirit. If He is active in the Council, the words "possible," "impossible," and "probable" lose their safe meanings. No one can say in advance what will come.

You ask: *"What do you see in the Council for the future of the Church; the reunion of the Christian churches; the progress of the Faith in the world?"* These are, surely, the three great areas of discussion; but it must be observed at once that they condition and influence one another rather considerably.

On the one hand, the face which the Catholic Church presents to the world determines to a large degree the chances of reunion of all the Christian churches. It is this very bond which the Holy Father has so precisely made between the work of the Council and that more remote intention, which in his thought the Council ought to aim at: to ponder the ways of a better union among Christians, and to consider the new and encouraging possibilities of their union. Doubtless the Council will take very seriously the immediate perspective of the work which is asked of it. Still, it is good, even for that purpose, for it to listen to the voices of those who, knowing well the sincere appeals of our separated brothers in the Orient and in the West, are called in conscience to express these appeals with all the measure and seriousness which the Church demands when she addresses herself to those separated persons. Something of this has been done already, for example, in Hans Küng's *The Council, Reform and Reunion* (Sheed & Ward, 1962). We can hardly have too much of this. Blessings on our Orthodox, Protestant, and Anglican brothers, who take it upon themselves to do this work!

Churchmen are well aware of the appeals of the non-Christian world; their pastoral office, with its many inquiries, makes them familiar with them. But it is not plain that pastors see their full extent and seriousness. A clerical formation has made them too used to seeing reasons for opposition only as objections or bad thinking, sometimes even as ill will, when compared with the classical statements of Catholic positions. And if we are to consider more serious difficulties, what churchman has met, even once, a real atheist? Has he ever left his world of certitudes? Has he ever gone into waters over his head? And isn't it true that a certain screen of convention and respectability has separated him from the genuine reactions of man? In my opinion, it is in this that the alarmingly ritualized part of our clerical life—its dress, habits of life, vocabulary, etc.—has its most serious defect. This hinders us, and the more so as we rise in the ecclesiastical hierarchy, from contact with men in those moments when they express themselves most freely. In front of us, they scarcely ever do this. The Church is the victim of her priestly cast, of the categories of thought, life, and *expression* which she has inherited from the centuries of the Roman Empire and of Christendom, and which she still wears just as the Swiss Guards still wear the helmets designed by Michaelangelo or as Danish pastors still wear the hats and ruffles of the age of Rembrandt.

Yes, the face which the Church shows is of vital importance if she is concerned with reuniting a world in which one man in four is Chinese, one man in three lives under a Communist regime and one Christian in two is not Catholic. When in 1935 my co-workers at *Les Éditions du Cerf* asked me to draw up a theological conclusion to the inquiry which they had been conducting for three years on the real causes of unbelief, I was led not only to formulate a unified interpretation,[1] but to reflect on what could be done. It seemed to me that *since the belief or unbelief of men depended so much on us,* the effort to be made was a renovation of ecclesiology. We must recover, in the ever-living sources of our profound tradition, a meaning and a face of the Church which will truly be that of the People of God—Body of Christ—Temple of the Holy Spirit. This

---

1 Cf. *La Vie Intellectuelle,* July 25, 1935.

conclusion led to the *Unam Sanctam* collection, (37 volumes to date) and the books which I have written myself: *Divided Christendom* (Bles, 1937), *Vraie et fausse réforme dans l'Église*,[2] *Lay People in the Church* (Newman), *Christ, Mary and the Church* (Newman), *The Mystery of the Temple* (Newman, 1962). About eight years ago I came to a new conclusion: it is not only our idea and our presentation of the Church which must be renewed in its source, it is our idea of God as a *living* God, and in the light of this, our idea of Faith. I shall return to this point later.

Of the three points of the above inquiry, the first deeply colors the other two, and the second affects the third. "May they be one so that the world may believe," Jesus said. Historically, the divisions among Christians, the fiercely cruel wars, carried out in the name of dogmatic differences, are largely responsible for the genesis of modern unbelief (Herbert of Cherbury, Spinoza, the *Philosophes* of the eighteenth century). Concretely, the division among Christians is a scandal for the world. The world is exonerated, to a degree, from the duty to believe.

But the above-mentioned conditioning works in both directions. The last two points of the inquiry profoundly condition the first. The future of the Catholic Church evidently depends on herself, on the dynamism which has been infused into her by her founder and teacher.[3] I believe that the future of the Church insofar as it is to be realized in history depends *also* on the fact that besides herself there are our separated brothers, and that directly confronting her is the world which is indifferent, hostile, or at least protesting and disturbing. I believe that *this* point is precisely significant for the present task of the Church, and she must do her utmost to recognize and pursue it at the Council.

It comes down to this—and all these current problems come down to this, I think: today the Church must be seen, not just in itself, but also in its mandate to the world and its relation to others, or in the relation of others to herself. The needs of the times have their center in this precise point: the Church exists in herself, by virtue of a foundation which does not come from history, but from the Lord. Nevertheless, she exists in the world, for the world: that which is said of her Lord is equally true of her: *Qui propter nos, homines, et propter nostram salutem, descendit....* Hence missions and ecumenism, the hearing of the Word and dialogue, the attention to appeals and to questions, are part of her existence as the Church of this world and the Church militant.

If the answer to this inquiry concerning the Church allows for such developments, I would here suggest two points for theological meditations.

---

2 This book has not appeared in English, but sections were translated in Cross Currents: "Attitudes Toward Reform in the Church" (Summer 1951), and "Vrai et fausse réforme" (Summer 1953).

3 Cf. *The Mystery of the Church* (Helicon).

1. Concerning the *catholicity* of the Church: I would point out that she must join in herself a source from above—the fullness of Christ—and a source from below: the fullness of creation, not as sluggish and stagnant, but alive, active in research, full of questions, in labor to "increase and multiply." The idea of "fullness" which St. Paul proposes in his Epistle to the Ephesians is then capable of two meanings: Christ completes, and is Himself completed (cf. 1, 23). The Church, then, makes the connection between Christ and the world. This point is, in my opinion, decisive. It marks a fundamental division between integralists and others, the former wanting everything in the Church to be determined from above. If only this "from above" were from Jesus Christ! But it is all too often a question of human representatives who do not have the same guarantees of universal fullness, or of "traditions" going back sometimes a few decades, sometimes to a past that is dead and gone.

2. Concerning the *temporality* of the Church, that is to say, her full earthly and militant character, her complete and true humanity, proceeding from the humanity of Jesus Christ, whose divine dignity it does not, incidentally, possess. What must be sought is genuine growth along the paths of history, which are those of opposition and strife, not just a harmonious development, ideally preserved by a purely internal flowering. Didn't St. Paul go so far as to write, *"Opportet haereses esse"*? It is necessary that there be the rending of divisions.

After these general considerations, I will take up again, very briefly, each of the three points of the above inquiry.

1. The Council's action will strongly commit the future of the Catholic Church. It will doubtless make a clear reaffirmation of the principles on which the Church has lived, lives now, and must always continue to live. In the face of the fundamental questioning which history has posed, the Church has always begun with a reaffirmation of her principles. This is a sign of life and health. Other steps present themselves as follows:

a) On the level of practical behavior. We have an occasion clearly to renounce, certainly not the task of influencing the temporal according to the will of God and towards God—that task is essential to the Church, and its urgency is not lessened today—but certain ways of acting by means of carnal power and earthly prestige. The Council must strive to help the Church find a way of being really and evangelically *present* in the great moments of human life. Many people today are seeking for a Church less *of* the world but more *in* the world. There is, to be sure, a bit of illusion in this request, which must be taken into account. Some dream of a Church which would be only prophecy, only message, since a message can be "pure." But the Church is an incarnation, and an incarnation is never completely "pure." Nevertheless, the Church must, in following Christ, seek an incarnation which would make her message

27

transparent. Today we must energetically seek for modes of existence in the Church—including the area of the exercise of authority—so that she may be seen as clearly as possible and to the highest degree as a *sign* of the Gospel. Such a sign can be accepted—consider the example of the Little Brothers of Jesus, or of Toumliline—and it is effective. This would be compliance with the gospel.

b) On an internal and profound level, that is, of doctrine and the Christian message itself, it is necessary, without giving up anything of the deposit of Faith developed by centuries of Christian life, to present a *simple* formulation of doctrine, centered on what is essential. In my opinion, the essential point to remember is that biblical and evangelical revelation is not, in its essential intention, a theoretical system, but an affirmation, simple and at the same time very rich, concerning what is the true religious relationship, that of man made in the image of God with the living God himself. In this revelation, there is never an affirmation about God which does not concern man, which does not call him into question, illuminate his situation, and call for a response from man to God, at the same time as God's gift of grace to sinful man. A contemporary Jewish author has written these words, which have profound meaning for those who understand them: "The Bible is not a theology for man; it is an anthropology for God." I think that it would be better to say that it is both, but never one without the other. One should never separate anthropology and *theo*-logy, not in order to humanize the latter, but to make it, in the thread of our lives, in both large and small events a living echo of the Word which God has communicated to us of Himself, so that we might live by it. For the God of revelation and of salvation is never more Himself than when He is so for man, in the thread of his human life. In my opinion this is the most important and urgent point of Christian preaching. The most damaging ambiguities and confusions come about when it is badly neglected.

If we understand this well, we shall easily recover the spirit of men conquered by Jesus Christ and devoted to His gospel, and we shall find the style of preaching and expression which is awaited by a world hungry for that gospel. This requires a rediscovery of the God of the Bible, the Living God. It leads to the reality of faith as a service to the living God, which takes nothing away from the intellectual aspects of that faith, but gives them their true status and their biblical fullness of meaning.

2) The reconciliation of the Christian churches requires an openness to a dialogue, without betraying the certitudes of dogma. The most delicate points in the initiatives to be taken arise from the new need to find out the *positive elements* in the requests of the Others. In the confrontation and final rupture between the Christians of the East and the West, in the dramatic revolt of the Reformers, there were not simply misunderstandings and negations; there were also positive requests which were finally affirmed in a different interpretation of Christianity as a

whole, and even, if one thinks of the Reformation, of the basic religious relationship. I think that the questions posed in this way will not be avoided, for it is precisely such questions which give the ecumenical dialogue its depth.

It is doubtless impossible that the Council will accomplish, in a few months, results that will attract the attention of several generations. But it can commit the Church to undertake the work under new conditions, better conditions than those under which many of our brothers have been working up to now. The creation of the Secretariat for Christian Unity, linked concretely with the private efforts which have been made along these lines for the last thirty years, is a promise that all have greeted as the most novel and the most fortunate preparatory step of the Council. As an example, I cite the Executive Committee of the Ecumenical Council of Churches, which in its meeting of August, 1960 quoted—and this touched me deeply—a phrase which I had written immediately after the announcement of the Council: "For the first time in history, the Catholic Church is entering into the structure of dialogue."

3) As for the progress of the faith in the world, I need not repeat what I have said in speaking of the future of the Catholic Church. I will only sketch three themes, which concern respectively the three worlds of our Catholic-ecumenical parish:

a) *The Marxist World.* Beyond condemnations and denials, some means must be found of an evangelical approach. Joseph de Maistre wrote in 1817, "Why another Council, when the pillory is enough?" Who would not consider that remark a bit curt? Now, without neglecting the philosophical, scientific, social, economic and human answers to the problems posed by Marxism, there is a field which can be an area of positive encounter: *the building of peace.* Let us hope that the Council truly accomplishes something to this end!

b) *As for the free world,* which is also, alas, a materialist world, more and more given to the search for material comfort, even in those parts of it which are amenable to moral values, it must be evangelized in depth. A new knighthood of Christian service must be raised up, a company of Christian witnesses.

c) *The neutral world* will largely determine, according to which side they support, the immediate future of the planet. We must investigate and honor their problems, as the encyclical *Mater et Magistra* invites us to do; we must give them voice and lead them to take a creative place in the Church, somewhat like the place taken, in their time, by the Greco-Roman and the Germanic world. But here I can only name and suggest the problem. To develop its implications would surpass the limits both of a response that is already too long and of my own competence.

translated by BARRY N. RIGNEY

John Julian Ryan

The Phoenix Arises

*I*nasmuch as a number of participants in this symposium have similar backgrounds, I propose to avoid a needless repetition by limiting myself to reflections derived primarily from my own experience, especially my experience as a teacher. However briefly, I wish to concern myself with the specific function of Catholic education in the contemporary world, and the forces that are inimical to it. It is also important for us to see that the Church unwittingly cooperates with, or at least fails adequately to combat, these forces; if this is clear, we will be in a better position to think about what the Council can do to help remedy this failure.

A preliminary statement of the aim of Catholic education may be stated in the following terms:—

It is to help the student acquire the various kinds of skill he requires in performing his all-encompassing vocation as a Christian. For the work of the Christian is twofold: the direct (explicit) worship of God (in the Mass, the sacraments, prayer, fasting, contemplation); and the indirect (implicit) worship of Him in all other activities (whether of play or of labor). The Catholic educator cannot be primarily concerned with turning out students who will be what most people today would call "successes," nor is he interested in giving them that veneer of culture typical of the "right people." The Catholic graduate is to be equipped to take his part in the history of the Redemption—in promoting the coming of that Kingdom for which he prays in the Our Father.

Specifically, this means that the student is to be aided to become as intelligent and as well-disciplined as he can be in participating in the Mass and the sacraments, in praying, contemplating, and bearing witness. But it would be a complete misunderstanding if this were to be read as if Catholic colleges should be seminaries, or its graduates displaced persons in modern secular society. If we are successful, the watertight compartments of religious and secular will be broken down in the day-to-day lives of students who have learned to sacramentalize their every action and instrument. It is because of this sense of wholeness that they should possess a positive drive to discover, explore, and meditate

John Julian Ryan is professor of English at St. Anselm's College, Manchester, N. H., and the author of IDEA OF A CATHOLIC COLLEGE *(Sheed and Ward) and* BEYOND HUMANISM *(Sheed and Ward). He and his wife, Mary Perkins Ryan, have pioneered in the liturgical movement in this country.*

on, as well as rejoice at, the beauty of all the truths of the liberal sciences and acquire the various skills they foster. Our hope must be that in the conduct of their personal, domestic, economic, political, scholarly and social affairs, they will act not only as inspired by grace, but also as habitually guided by the intellectual virtues. And if we have really trained our students, they will go on growing, throughout their whole lives, in knowledge and skill.

Obviously, since the student's way of life depends on his hierarchy of values, and since he acquires this almost unconsciously—by, as it were, osmosis—one of the basic necessities is that the atmosphere of the Church, the climate of his spiritual life, be propitious. It will be extremely dangerous if he comes to feel that the Church is made up of the acquisitive, the philistine, the literal-minded, the legalistic, the bourgeois.

If that happened, he might mistakenly assume that the proper motivation of a Christian is fear—whether of poverty, of the imagination, of insecurity, or of risk—all founded on distrust of God's loving providence and man's basic decency. He will then come to believe that the Catholic Church should not commit itself *positively*—and therefore *inspiringly*—to anything much; and certainly it should show no preferences in matters temporal. After all, a banker, an industrialist, or an advertising man can save his soul; let us, therefore, not be "too hasty" in condemning such occupations; *and,* therefore, let us do nothing much about changing them. If the Church accepts these things—as it seems to do—how can one seriously raise questions as to the possibility of supplanting usurious banking with non-usurious, or mass production with humane quantity production, or manipulative advertising with sound persuasion?

Of course, the Church cannot go in for virulent demagoguery, and violent change—even when justifiable—may prove more harmful than not. But it must equally be concerned about being an ally of any temporary system, and should guard against promoting its cause as being in the interests of the home, of democracy, or of anything else. If it is a mistake—as it is—for a family to pray together mainly in order to stay together, it is no less a mistake to promote the cause of the Church as a bulwark against Communism. For, as St. Augustine has pointed out, sin consists in enjoying what should be used and in using what should be enjoyed. To combat Communism in order to enjoy freedom of worship is one thing; to use the Church so as to enjoy freedom from Communism is something else again. And so for all other goods that are meant to be "added" unto us. In short, it is wise for the Church never to get so involved in a particular worldly affair as to be finally identified with it.

But to grant all this is not to grant that ultimate and basic truths (beyond and above all particular principles) and all fundamental motives and norms cannot be dynamic and inspiring. The Church can always exercise great force simply by making it clear to the Christian what it is natural for him to do as a Christian. It can make quite clear to a baker, let us say, whether he should obey the law of supply and demand and charge more for a loaf of bread the more his patron needs it—or not. The saints have seldom been noted as great casuists; yet somehow they seem to have known what principles to follow in particular circumstances, and—they seem to have been inspired to follow them at whatever sacrifice.

Indeed, the norms of Christian living are far more determinable, without committing us to an ideology, than we are inclined to admit. For instance, it is clear from the Bible that the first view we are to have of God and of man is as makers; the one, a super-eminent Maker, a loving Creator, Whose wisdom *"played* before Him"; the other, as one charged to "dress the garden" of paradise. What, then, is it more "natural" for the Christian to be than a co-worker with God, one of His sons, who serves others skilfully and charitably—according to the motive made clear to him by Christ in the washing of the feet on Holy Thursday and the death on the Cross on Good Friday? And what is more "natural" for a group of Christians who are concerned with providing fellow members of society with some one means of leading Christian lives than that they should band together to form an association in which they share their knowledge and fix the conditions of justice and charity for the ensuring of good work? And what is more "natural" to a society wishing to promote general peace, prosperity and neighborly generosity than that it should try to assure to everyone, not just the professional man, a life of trained, dedicated, charitable service?

Surely an ideal like this is, for the Christian, in the very nature of things. And the norms it proposes are neither too narrowly ideological nor too vaguely general; at the least, they lead to a firm and deliberate rejection of unsound policies. How, for instance, in the light of them, can a Christian be content with an industrialism, whether capitalist or communist, that first degrades craftsmen to the level of mere workers or "hands" and then preens itself on affording them a "just" wage and the treatment of a good race-horse? Is it possible, in charity, to deprive a man of the right and joy of being a dedicated artist who uses meritoriously his two specifically human powers, his will and intellect? How can one rest content with any system of publicity or propaganda, whether capitalist or communist, which manipulates the subconscious mind to trap the conscious into impulsive, sub-rational action? The very least the Church can do, then, is help Christians to feel, not a tepid but a burning abhorrence of systems that run counter to man's nature as seen by the Bible and the liturgy, as well as a positive preference for systems that accord with that nature.

Granted that it is necessary to make haste slowly; that in matters of opinion, custom, or particular technique the Church should not take sides; that every norm should be obeyed flexibly and tactfully—still, there are obviously some economic, social and political arrangements more consonant than others with the requirements of heroic Christian living as a member of the Mystical Body of Christ. There are some that are less suited to the self-centered, the acquisitive, the shrewd, the pseudo-conservative (who conserves primarily what is to his own advantage), and the pusillanimous, and more suited to the generous, the magnanimous, the truly prudent, the poetic, the heroic and the saintly. It is these norms, therefore, which the Church must promulgate positively and eloquently, in accordance with the spirit in which Our Lord said that He had come to set the world on fire and to pit brother against brother.

The present Council would do well then, it seems to me, to reassert the dynamic truths (and to reassert them dynamically), of the religion of generosity, heroism, and joy, and to call on everyone, from Cardinal to janitor, to bear witness that the Catholic Church is the Church of the open mind, the open heart, the open hand—the mother of heroes. It should do so, not only to erase the opposite impression, now all too prevalent, both inside and outside the Church, but also to attract or hearten all those who wish to lead heroically generous lives—the "good ground," the salt of the earth.

Further, the Council would do well to bear witness, itself, by its very style of utterance, to the fact that the Church is the Church of the "heart," in the biblical, especially the Pauline, sense of the word. God the Father has spoken to us, His children, through the Prophets and His Son, in the language of poetry. He expects to be thought of, appreciated, prayed to, in terms of this language. Might not the Council say as much expressly and then, by their own speech, testify to their Christ-like distaste for literal-mindedness and legalistic frigidity? If it is all right to say to a scholar that "grace is created actuation by uncreated act," it is better to speak of grace to everyone else as food that nourishes the starving, water that cleanses and quenches, oil that soothes and strengthens, health that frees from paralysis and restores the sight, life that raises from the dead. To say that "a worker should be given a fair wage" is not incorrect; but it is far more Christian to say, "One of the four sins that cry to Heaven for vengeance—along with sodomy, wilful murder, and the cheating of widows and children—is the failure to pay your helper a just wage." If, as Pius XII pointed out, we are all spiritually Semites, should we not also be so stylistically? Maybe the Council can speak less in the mode of a Renaissance Cicero and more in the mode, in this Apocalyptic era, of St. John.

Then, when the Phoenix arises, purged of the dirt and parasites of many years, she will take once more to the heights freely, radiantly. And the Council will have fulfilled the momentous task which Pope John proposed for it at the outset—that of "giving back to the face of the Church the splendor of the simpler and purer form of her birth."

Georges Mollard

A Parish Priest

A parish priest for thirty years, I await the forthcoming Council as a Pentecost, an evangelical return to the sources for the universal Church, which will deeply affect the life of the humblest parish and the religious experience of each Christian.

I will speak from the viewpoint of my experience as a parish priest, but this does not mean that I will limit myself to specifically parochial questions. I am both a priest and a man; I feel a deep solidarity both with the whole Church and with the city of man. I will try to say how a curé sees the problem posed today for the Church by the world or, if you prefer, how he sees the mission of the Church in today's world; this will permit me to affirm the spiritual aspect of the various concrete proposals for reform which I will try to present.

According to what the Pope has said and what is known of the preliminary work, the Council seems to be centered on a concern for unity and a more evangelical religious life in the Church. These two concerns are connected and imply both a deepening of a living faith and a greater spirit of openness.

In fact, the general climate of the Catholic Church since the Reformation has been defensive and protective: it has withdrawn to its fortress position; it has lived within itself, sheltered from exterior contagion, in a framework of strict discipline. This had its justification and was beneficial at a particular period, but its continuance has had unfortunate consequences for the Church, which are evident even on the level of parish life. I will mention three of them:

a) By the very fact that it has retrenched, the Church is no longer in a position fully to accomplish its mission in the world. (Every curé has noticed that the parish community tends to constitute a bloc that appears alien to the ordinary life of men.)

b) Pastoral experience suggests that Christians live a feeble religious life, too much enclosed in Church forms and insufficiently initiated in the mystery of Christ.

c) Evangelical inquiry and apostolic initiative are often suspect; dialogue, necessary for the harmony of initiative and discipline, is always difficult and frequently impossible; an infantile mentality of resignation

---

Father Georges Mollard is a parish priest in Grenoble, France.

is confused with the virtue of obedience and paralyzes the spirit at its source.

The Council, however, considers the search for Unity as axiomatic. Thus it looks beyond the frontiers of the Roman Church and locates itself in a framework of openness.

I hope to see the Council pursue the demands of this openness of spirit to the utmost. It would be regrettable if the Roman Church emerged from its retrenchment only to lock itself in a new ghetto, as in a Christian bloc against non-Christian religions, or against the world.

I hope, therefore, that the Council will inaugurate an era of dialogue, not only with our Christian brothers of other confessions, but also with all who worship God—Jews, Moslems, Hindus. They have many values in common with our own and their rich religious experience ought to become a good shared by all. (As a French priest I must take note of the religious values brought to us by workers from North Africa.)

More important still, I await the beginning of dialogue between the Church and the world; this would suppose, on the Church's part, a profound sympathy for humanity, which is proceeding in great pain on the march toward unity, starving for justice and peace. Here are sure signs for us of a fermentation in which the spirit of God is in travail.

But evidently, if the Church is to become truly present in the world —a world that is strong, in a state of constant expansion, whose mystique is often intoxicated—this will place an absolute demand upon Christians for an increased, interior, spiritual strength, with an emphasis upon a clarified and living faith, nourished by the word of God and sustained by the fraternal warmth of association.

Let me try to be more concrete regarding this double movement of growing deeper roots in the faith and of opening out to enfold more of reality.

I

To Accept the World Without Reticence, and Love It

In baptism the priest baptizes the child whom its parents made. He accepts it as it is.

This should be a pattern of our acceptance of the world as it is, without reticence and without regret; even better, with love, growing from a discovery of its worth. We are to receive it with love, although aware of its sin; at least we are not to condemn it from outside, as if we were pure, but to support it and suffer with it as with our own sinning existence. Out of many possibilities, let me draw implications from this:

1) We must accept the fact that a very great part of the expanding world is socialist, not only in political structures but in the new kind of man it is creating. This socialist man is beloved of God and has the right to live by his word.

35

2) We must accept the fact that the whole world—whether capitalist, socialist, or neutralist, is an adult, fully autonomous world which will refuse, simply by virtue of its human dignity, any religious paternalism offered in the name of the "Christian order."

Such a world is to be accepted, respected, loved; its conscience must be addressed from within.

The Presence of the Church in the World

From the viewpoint of the parish priest the problem is one of parish and neighborhood. We priests have much harm to undo from the old spirit of Christendom; instinctively we tend to build up a little Christian city (formerly the city as parish, today the parish community) within the larger city of men. We must have *our* charitable works, *our* organizations, *our* schools, *our* men's groups. In these we spend our time, much money, and admirable devotion. But in them we lose our freedom, our joy in living, and sometimes even our religious life.

We must become convinced that the Christian life led in such conditions is a survival from the past and that it cannot support the evangelical ferment in the world at large for the very simple reason that such a Christian life is a retrenchment.

We must accept the fact that Christians live their whole human life in the world at large outside the framework of the Church. They work; it is not our job to form Christian shops, or Christian unions to defend their rights. They need relaxation; it is not for us to organize Christian leisure activities, or a Christian political party, or Christian family associations.

Christians, who are by no means set apart from others, will live their lives like all other men, confronting all the problems of their time and of their milieu with a conscience clarified by faith and animated by charity.

Is this to say that the Church as such will have no role to play in society? Absolutely not.

It will have no directly political role, true; but, on the one hand, by refraining from constantly providing a total environment in which Christians are to make their commitments, the Church can devote itself entirely to sustaining and animating their faith. On the other hand —and this is very important—*when the Christian congregation is no longer compromised within institutions, it will become free and strong enough to take courageous positions of collective conscience in the face of human problems.*

Doubtless it is necessary to control the stages of liberation from the vestiges of official Christendom, but I hope that the Council will orient itself toward a certain separation between the Church and so-called Christian temporal structures—political parties, Christian democracy, unions—and that it will recognize the full value of Christian commitment to non-confessional institutions, with the understanding that this presence is undertaken with the desire simply to cooperate in the public good.

The Church, Money, Capitalism, Socialism

There has been a great deal of talk about "the clink of money around the altar";[1] many priests have accepted significant sacrifices for the sake of necessary purification. To continue along such lines is certainly evangelically correct. It is necessary, too, that parish or diocesan finances be clearly and publicly explained; even honestly administered secret funds must be renounced. St. Paul's handling of gifts received for Jerusalem must serve as our example.

All this is necessary and is entirely accepted by many priests, but we must go further. Can the Council, after a long era of capitalism, not assess the fundamental opposition between Christianity and an economy based on profit?

Certainly the Church did not create capitalism; it pursued its mission despite the anti-evangelical basis of capitalism; it was correct in palliating, as best it could, the evils which capitalism fatally engendered. But today, after a century of association which has not failed to leave its mark upon the Church and, to use St. Paul's word, to "blemish" it, would it not be well if the Council withdrew a little so as to purify the Church from its capitalist stains and to loosen the ties of fact (certainly not of right) which associate the Church with capitalism? (Examples from the parish level include compromise with business management for Church building or the financing of Christian schools, etc., with its corollary, the unemployed who ask the parish priest for job recommendations.)

Inversely, while guarding against any marriage of the Church to socialism, Christians who have chosen a socialist economy as more rational and more humane should no longer be considered suspect in their faith, but should be made fully at home in the Christian congregation. This assumes more than simple tolerance; this demands that the Church recognize the value of the great human movement toward justice and peace which is allied to the advent of socialism; this demands, too, that the Church in its declarations not speak, as it were, from inside capitalism to curb its abuses but that it also place itself in a position to *judge socialism from within.*

We must try to determine the degree to which the priest's apostolic influence is limited by the fact that he appears in his parish not enough

---

[1] Cf. the much-discussed book of Abbé Michonneau, *Revolution in a City Parish* (Newman).

as a man of faith, a man of Christ and the gospel, and too much as a man of "the right," a supporter of the established order, on easy terms with the rich.

And if this is true within the narrow limits of the parish, it is much more so in the wider scope of the world. The bond of fact between the Church and capitalism helps to give the Church the aspect of a state religion supporting the reigning economy; beyond the frontiers of the capitalist world the Church is too easily seen as an export product or as propaganda.

Laymen

I am not a layman and I am embarrassed to speak for laymen. But the frank statements of militant Christians, from all backgrounds, have much in common. Two points constantly recur:

1) The Church is always speaking to us about adult faith, but it treats us like children.

Because of their faith, laymen acknowledge the authority of the hierarchy and its power of instruction and jurisdiction, but they also believe, because of this same faith, in the grace of their baptism and their confirmation, which makes them adult members of the Church.

For them, the authentic life of the Church presupposes the existence of dialogue between the hierarchy and the people of God, a necessary element if the hierarchy is to know in their living reality the problems of the Christian conscience and necessary, too, if the layman's obedience is to be a strong act of free conscience.

I ask my brother-priests and my superiors, the bishops, not to believe too easily that they are listening to laymen because they receive them and let them talk. For a laymen to express himself he must be convinced that he is being listened to as a vital, active member of the Church of Christ, who also (in his place, and always under possible illusions) is animated by the spirit of God. The priest must not listen to the layman as to one who gives information only, but as to a son of God, living by the Holy Spirit. To listen to laymen is to be eavesdropping on God.

2) Laymen, in the same sense, would like the Council to reconsider the very concept of Catholic Action.

Catholic Action has been defined as lay participation in the apostolate of the hierarchy; the theory of its mandate derives from this.

Laymen understand that the roots of their missionary vocation lie in their baptism and confirmation much more deeply than in episcopal mandate.

Courage is needed to confront the very grave crisis which Catholic Action is undergoing; the crisis can be surmounted only through recognition of the worth of the baptized Christian as a fully adult member

of the Church. Only by ridding the movement of all clerical paternalism can the indispensable authority of the hierarchy be maintained in
full strength.

I hope that the Council, in order to eavesdrop on the spirit of God
in travail in the soul of all baptized, will elicit many testimonies from
laymen. They should not be satisfied with testimony only from permanent members of Catholic Action committees who are too conditioned
by their functions, which cut them off, at least partially, not only from
the world, but also from the Christian people.

Priests

The Council will certainly touch on the problem of the priesthood,
a difficult problem, because even we priests often have trouble in defining ourselves.

The priest fulfills ritual functions but, unlike his role in the Old
Testament, his ministry does not stop there. The priest is also the minister of the word and has charge of souls: wherever there is a Christian
community there must be a priest to announce the Word of God, cele-
brate the eucharistic sacrifice and effect the "cure" of souls.

But is this enough to say? Wherever the priest has been sent, he
deeply feels himself to be the priest, not only to Christians but to *all:*
he has at heart all those who live in his parish; he must bear witness
of the gospels to them, and pray for them.

Canonical rule, the manner of life imposed upon the priest, and recent decisions of the Roman Congregations, seem to bind the priest
firmly within a Christian community. But although he is assigned to
a community, he ought not to be enclosed by it; he ought, rather, to be
a sign of Christ for all. I will be told, certainly, that the whole Christian community must give such a sign. True, but the priest, in the
first rank of his community, is a sign for all.

If we admit that the priest, the minister of the sacraments and the
one who animates his community's spiritual life, is also *the first witness of the community for those outside it,* it will have great consequences for both his religious practice and for his style of life.

For his religious practice. The religious malaise of parish priests is
well known; they are inwardly divided by the practical incompatibility
between the semi-monastic spiritual life learned in the seminary and
ministerial duties in the world at large. The basis of the priest's spiritual life ought to be in the exercise of his ecclesiastical functions and,
I underline, in *charity among a whole people.*

For his style of life. According to St. Paul, he is to be all things to
all men in order to win all for Jesus Christ. This certainly does not
mean an isolated life (although from some viewpoints it may be said
that the priest is isolated, this does not imply that he must lead *an*

isolated life) but a sharing in the human condition in life's concrete reality, not only in spirit.

To decide what is meant by the true presence of a priest to *all* his people, one must free himself from old habits, normal in "Christian countries" but unadaptable in very many places. I will explain:

For all practical purposes, in an earlier age of Christendom, parish and community were mingled, and by his ministry, which extended to all and so isolated him from none, the priest had in fact human roots by virtue of his sacred duties themselves.

In a community or neighborhood today the parish may represent only eight to ten percent of the population; in the workers' suburbs or the new cities, often less than three percent. The priest who lets himself become absorbed by religious service to the Christian community alone is no longer available to the whole people and no longer has human roots; he is uprooted from true human life. There is no other reason for the deep and general uneasiness among the young clergy and for the crisis regarding vocations for the priesthood. Only by accepting these very positive grounds (the concrete life offered to a man who remains *a man* while making a gift of his life to the service of Christ, the Church, and his brothers in the Catholic priesthood) can we meaningfully take up the problems everywhere raised today in regard to the priest: his habit, his work, and the possibility of married priests.

1) The priest's habit

In my opinion, the question of wearing a cassock is wholly dependent upon the priest's situation in a given environment. There is no need to abandon the cassock in an area of Christendom. Besides, why leave it off if the priest is to remain enclosed in his little parochial cell? But, obversely, why hold on to the cassock at all costs where it might hinder the possibility of bearing an evangelical witness? It is all a question of environment.

I cannot say as much for certain ceremonial costumes. I speak respectfully and freely, because it is clear that many bishops, and obviously, the Pope, are profoundly humble and bear the weight of honors without complacency. But it must be placed in evidence by every priest who does what he can to listen to both Christians and non-Christians: ecclesiastical pomp does much harm; along with money it is one of the obstacles to the faith; it makes many say, "I believe in Jesus Christ but not in the Church."

Let bishops and cardinals give up their violet and red and wear the same cassock as priests; let them renounce the titles of Eminence and Excellency and be called "Mister" like everyone else. No more miters, and pectoral crosses; let us suppress the idea of monsignors and canons. What has the gospel to do with all that?

If the Pope was made aware of the harm done by his court, which the most faithful and loving of his sons feel to be a family disgrace, he would not be long in sending the Swiss guard back home, along with the porters of the *sedia;* he would free himself of the intolerable burden of his museums by making a gift of his treasures to some international institution.

If the Council enters upon this path, which after all demands no great courage, it will be sustained by the immense approbation of Christian people, approbation of quite another kind from the kissing of bishops' rings or applause in the piazza of St. Peter's.

A Christian friend once said to me, "When medicine became serious, doctors knew that it was useless to disguise themselves; the Church will some day accept in its heart only what is serious."

2) *Work for priests*

It is from the point of view of the need of the priest for human roots, and his presence among a whole people that one should speak of work for priests.

It is not because of fashion, or lack of occupation, or, still less, distaste for sacred functions, that curés and vicars have gone to work, within permitted limits, and earn at least a part of their livelihood. Through work they create, at least partially, a living tie with a whole population whose priests they feel themselves to be; they make their priesthood respected by the workers, who believe that human dignity lies in work; and they reveal clearly to everyone their means of subsistence.

In the same sense in which, as a parish priest, I know very well that even if I earn my living my possibilities of influence are greatly limited by my strict parochial ties, so it must be acknowledged that in fact the parochial communities of France are recruited from a thoroughly determined sociological milieu—in the cities, the middle class. It must be acknowledged that for the moment, with only individual exceptions, we cannot hope to see factory workers integrated into these parishes. For example, a construction worker whom I know well, whose faith I know to be real and vital, came only once to our church, for his daughter's communion. As he left he told me, "It was good, but I constantly had the feeling that I was betraying my kind."

Let us not get irate over such a state of mind. If the proletariat were in the majority in our churches, we would have another problem. The Church is willing to give parishes to chaplains and foreigners and sees no threat to unity in doing so; it merely recognizes an actual situation and tries to meet it. Let us have the same courage to see the Church in France as it is and state the clear limits of its sociological implantation. This will impose the necessity of liberating priests, of loosening their ties with existing communities, so that they may be, in the whole world of work—and therefore as workers—witnesses to the gospel.

41

In conclusion, concerning the cassock, work for the priest, and the worker-priest, I hope that the Council will leave great freedom of judgment to the bishops. The priesthood is lived within a people and for a people; the manner of the priest's human life must be decided according to his people.

3) Married priests

The conventional Christian and the militant Christian have a very different approach to the problem of the marriage of priests. Let me say immediately that it would completely falsify the question if the state of marriage for the priest were considered as a surrender, a "cut-rate" priesthood. Some committed Christians would like to see the priest in a position to assume religiously the totality of their lives; since family life is one of the major elements of their lives as human beings and Christians, they would like the priest to be able to assume it too. This attitude is not to be confused with contempt for ecclesiastical celibacy; this represents another set of values to be assumed. They certainly are not asking that all priests get married; they ask only that there be married priests.

I would be glad if the Council would reintroduce the ancient usage of ordaining married men, on condition that they are not considered priests of a second rank. If they were truly the equals of celibate priests, they would help to renew dialogue between clergy and people, especially if they kept up a professional activity.

But I would guard against approaching this problem under the minor aspect of a means to remedy the lack of priests. Ordination of married men must be no facile solution to the crisis in recruiting the clergy but rather a response of the Church to a religious need of our time.

II

The Word of God

To live by its faith and to bear witness to the gospel in the whole world, the Christian people needs the word of God. Today a privileged few take nourishment from the Bible, but the Christian people does not have access to it.

To give the word of God to the people, the simplest and most normal means seems to me to be the liturgical assembly. But this would require recasting the first part of the mass.

We must bear in mind that a faithful Christian participant in the Sunday mass never hears a reading from the Old Testament; he is completely ignorant of the prophets. Every year he will listen to the same fifty-two fragments of the gospel in which are found neither the parable of the prodigal son, nor the resurrection of Lazarus, nor the story of the Samaritan woman.

Relatively easy reform might bear on two points:

Biblical prayer, the psalms: restoring the introit psalm, which today is reduced to one verse. I would like to replace the silent prayers at the altar with the recitation or singing of a psalm by the whole congregation.

Bible reading: for each Sunday, provision could be made of several passages from the Old Testament, the epistles, and the gospels; the celebrant would choose readings from among those texts. Preaching could then be biblical, at the same time that it would be renewed. Better still, to guide the priest's choice several series of epistle and gospel readings could be provided, for Advent, Lent, etc.

What is important is that the people of God live by the Bible.

A Liturgy Understood and Lived

The liturgy is more than the expression of our feelings; it is the celebration of the mystery of Christ and his Church. Before participating in the mystery and faithfully communicating in it, the Christian congregation must understand it.

Today's Christians want to understand what is said and done, what they say and sing themselves; they want to understand without dictionary and translation. (If you would like to measure how inadequate translation is for true comprehension, ask Christians the meaning of the *Tantum ergo,* which they have sung hundreds of times. You will be instructed.)

It seems to me very desirable to introduce *progressively* the use of the living language into the liturgy. It would not be suitable to do so wholesale, because some liturgical texts are untranslatable. When this is so, it is precisely because they are shaped by the mentality of the epoch in which they were composed, a mentality no longer our own. (In the Vespers for All Saints' Day, we sing, *Auferte gentem perfidam credentium de finibus,* which Dom Lefebvre faithfully translates, "Expel the infidel race from the borders of the believers." This had to do with the Normans, I have been told.)

Introducing the living language into the liturgy will pose problems, problems involved with our lives; constant revision of texts and rituals will be required. Certainly, we must not overturn everything, for it is the same Church which celebrates Christ's mysteries down through the centuries; we must make only the necessary adaptations that will enable today's Church, made up of men of today, truly to take part in the Mysteries.

To those who wish to keep the Latin for reasons of unity, I answer that the Church's unity lies in the faith and not in the language. Moreover, if an important part of the liturgy is celebrated in the living language, Christians will willingly accept recitation or singing of certain prayers in Latin (I would prefer Greek, for unity) as a sign of catholicity.

Restoring the Pastoral Meaning of the Sacraments

Here I approach a very difficult and grievous problem which I hope the Council can face courageously.

We administer the sacraments as if we lived in a Christian country, although only a minority of the population is Christian. In this way, though the sacraments remain true in themselves, their administration becomes false.

The harm is so widespread that too many examples come to mind. I will say only that since I became a priest I have baptized 5000 children. Except for very rare cases, the parents conducted themselves well, observed the proprieties, but (parish baptism occurs almost always on Sunday) not one time out of ten did the godfather, godmother, or the parents hear mass that day. In such a case we baptize though we know very well that the child will grow up in a virtually a-religious environment. Much the same can be said for confirmations, the first communions of children, and marriages.

Why do so many parents ask for baptism for their children and solemn communion for their boys and girls? Why do so many engaged couples wish to marry in the Church? Social pressure plays a considerable role: one must do as everyone else does, "according to the rules."

The consequences are very grave. The most serious is *contempt for religion,* which does not seem serious. In too rare moments of sincerity some people have said to us, "You don't believe in what you are doing." They were right—can a true faith in the sacraments be satisfied with the way in which they are administered?

Another consequence is a profound distortion of the people's understanding of religion. When performing rituals or acting in accord with a religious code involves no question of faith, religion is empty. All parish priests can give evidence of this emptiness in regard to death, where it is dazzlingly clear; there is great respect for death but a total absence of faith. Only the rites are asked of the priest.

A last, very serious consequence is that in making lifelong, empty religious gestures the priest destroys himself. Just as baptism or marriage celebrated in the faith can fortify a priest's faith, so daily ritual formalism can disintegrate his religious life.

Many priests have made immense efforts to restore vitality to desiccated ritualism, by visits to families before baptism, preparation of fiancés for marriage, etc. The results are deceptive (after the marriage the couple is never seen again) and this is understandable: it is good to assist a family which believes in the faith to perform the baptism of their first-born in the faith; it is our duty to assist fiancés who believe in the faith to be married in Christ; but it is false to proceed from preparation for the sacraments to a discovery of faith. This goes completely contrary to the practice of the apostles, who first preached salvation through the Christ, who died and rose again, and then gave baptism to those who believed.

This is not a question of severity, for the Church is made up of sinners, who need mercy. It is a question of truth that the sacraments be asked for, given, and received in faith.

Though I cannot be precise about the needed reform, I think that the crux of the investigation should be defined in this way: those who believe, mediocre and sinful as they may be, should have free access to the sacraments, while those who do not believe should not even ask for them.

What do I propose concretely? The evil is so widespread and so deep that small changes cannot cure it; the pastoral theology of the sacraments must be reformulated so as to reestablish their truthful administration in countries which have a pagan majority even though a religious folklore has been preserved.

Minor suggestions would include, without making a rule of it, letting children be only 'inscribed' on Catholic registries, postponing their baptism until they give a personal sign of faith. All that contributes to social pressure in solemn communion or marriage formalities can be pruned away; the ritual can be very sober, very spare.

I hope that more radical reforms will come from the Council so as to free the administration of the sacraments from these grievous ills.

I await the Council in hope and I will welcome its decisions in faith.

translated by ELIZABETH STAMBLER

The Concerns of Italian Laymen

Truth, Hierarchy, and Believers

The Catholics of our time generally agree on the existence of certain basic facts so far as the relations between Truth and the Church are concerned. Every Catholic would agree, for example, that the Church has a mandate from Christ to teach the gospel and make it manifest in the world through the lives of its members. None would deny that it is the hierarchy's responsibility to safeguard the purity and integrity of the evangelical message, despite various interpretations and disagreements over the generations. In short, every Catholic, from the least informed layman to the most learned theologian, must accept the authority of the hierarchy with explicit and respectful confidence when it is exerted to defend, clarify or solicit, to restrain or refute.

However unanimous this agreement among Catholics may be in theory, it turns out to be a different matter as soon as concrete issues are taken up. Catholics—and we are speaking particularly of Italian Catholics whom we know best—frequently disown each other as soon as there are choices in which they are directly involved. Though they may be expressed as categorical affirmations, these repudiations are often nothing but arbitrary interpretations or deductions of principles which are derived from doctrine.

We should also take into account the tendency to use declarations of the hierarchy for the sole purpose of borrowing support for one's personal choices, simultaneously attacking the positions of others, whether divergent or contrary, even if they possess a certain probability. Some even do not hesitate to pass off as "directives" of the hierarchy—with a reminder of its infallibility—private statements by eminent men, whose words certainly ought to be heard with attention and respect, but who have not been charged to commit the Church in this area, or direct the assent of the individual Christian.

This joint text appeared in the Italian magazine, LA MISSIONE, no. 28, 1960. It was issued by a group of Genoese Catholics working with the IL GALLO group. They describe themselves as "a group of eleven friends from fifty to sixty years old: a housewife, three workers, a clerk, an executive, a government employee, a public service employee, a secondary school teacher and two university graduates." They make it clear that they are not attempting to deal with doctrinal matters, but simply expressing their experience as militant Catholics.

What makes matters worse is the docile and unquestioning accept-ance, in the name of filial obedience, of anything with an official stamp, including articles which happen to appear in an official publication or talks by the heads of organizations at official Catholic functions. All this is encouraged, of course, by that "exaggerated authoritarianism" mentioned in the Italian Bishops' Joint Pastoral Letter on laicism, March 25, 1960. One segment of the laity responds to this exaggerated authoritarianism with passive, mechanical obedience, while others find themselves in a state of perpetual tension which leads either to silence or lame indifferentism. This tension is generally not manifested by open acts of rebellion, but rather by stray impulses of revolt and intermittent crises of conscience, which have a negative effect on the thoughts and actions of Catholics experiencing them. This is what happens in today's world, where the phenomenon of dechristianization takes many unpre-dictable forms, and where man is making efficient use of the means and gifts God has put at his disposal to "master the earth" (*Genesis* 1, 28).

But we cannot wholly blame modern Catholicism for a situation which has existed for centuries. It was perhaps a desire to clarify and remedy this situation which prompted the Vatican Council to approve the defi-nition of papal infallibility on July 16, 1870. It was an attempt to spell out how, and to what extent, the pope is infallible; in other words, it specifies at what moment and in what areas individual Catholics can exercise their own judgment.

Students of theology and canon law have perhaps not given sufficient attention to understanding the full meaning of the 1870 definition. An examination of its spirit and the heated discussion which led to its for-mulation would be useful. There is no doubt of its tendency to define and emphasize clearly, on one hand, the infallibility of the ecclesiastical magisterium, and on the other, the freedom of thought of Catholics in the immense domain untouched by infallibility.

This is not to say that those who have studied the question up to now have accomplished nothing. But laymen have known so little of their work that many of them have been content with mechanical obe-dience. They avoided any effort of reflection, interpretation and "intelli-gent respect," because they are convinced that the Christian's first duty is unconditional obedience. The result is an increasing withdrawal of many Catholics from any serious thinking on religious subjects.

It should be added that this retreat involves a renunciation of respon-sibility—which was precisely given emphasis in the Pastoral Letter. Many Catholics now tend to let all responsibility fall on the shoulders of the hierarchy and the clergy, as though the primary and absolute value of individual conscience constantly upheld by Catholic doctrine, and re-affirmed by certain theologians, has now been lost. The theological state-ment is clear:

The Church considers the problem of the individual conscience so important that she has instructed her doctors to proclaim the following principle: in the exceptional case where a religious authority—whether priest, bishop, or even pope—should order a Catholic to act against his conscience, the Catholic should refuse obedience, even if threatened with the gravest ecclesiastical sanctions. In the middle ages, Peter Lombard was widely opposed for attempting to express a contrary opinion, even though he was a teacher of unquestionable learning. On the other hand, Thomas Aquinas, Bonaventure, and doctors of the Church closer to modern times, as well as canon law itself, have reaffirmed the absolute value of conscience.[1]

It is in order to overcome this irresponsibility and to make the action of Christians at an extremely complex moment in history more efficacious that we point out to the Fathers of the Council the need for a clear and simple "instruction" on this fundamental and essential point of doctrine. We are not asking for new doctrines or new articles of canon law. The essential need is for a clarification of already-existing definitions and articles:

——the meaning and extent of the infallibility of the pope and of the Church;

——the varying degrees of authority in declarations on "faith and morals": from *ex cathedra* definitions to the declarations of each bishop, of pastors or parish assistants, of all those—be their pronouncements written or oral—who work in an apostolic group recognized by the hierarchy;

——the extent to which an agreement is binding should be proportionate to the degree of authority;

——the probable is an area of genuine scope and content and cannot be enlarged or diminished by partisan passions, whether intellectual, political or economic;

——Christian charity requires that, in attacking the arguments of Catholics who do not agree with us, we avoid insults, sarcasm, and other devices of partisan passion;

——all Catholics are bound by charity to reject both "exaggerated authoritarianism" and blind, mechanical obedience;

——the first and indispensable sign of love and respect for the hierarchy is to listen attentively to its pronouncements. We should attempt to understand and interpret them dispassionately, while reverently and freely making our own observations, should the occasion arise, since Christians have a vocation to freedom (*Galatians* 5, 13) and the Church

---

[1] Otto Karrer, *Die Freiheit des Christenmenschen* (Benziger). Also see J. Dargent, S.J., *Quelques principes de la Morale* (Lille, 1906); Johannes Hessen, *Luther in oekumenischer Sicht* (Bonn, 1947); P. de Lorson, S.J., *Un chrétien peut-il être objecteur de conscience?* (Paris, 1950).

is the body of Christ, not a pseudo-spiritual and totalitarian mechanism of thought and custom;

——in sum, Christians must be reminded of the primacy of conscience. If we really want the gospel to breathe life into this world in gestation, the individual conscience must not abdicate in the face of all that is mechanical and organized in the world of technology.

Hierarchy, Priesthood, and Laity in the Church

All that has just been said is closely connected with problems affecting the very life and nature of the Church, the relations of Catholics among themselves, and the relationship between the Church and the world. A hundred years ago these problems were not raised; the Church seemed to rest securely on solutions confirmed by centuries of experience. These problems were not seen with the scope and sharpness which they now have in the eyes of modern Christians, who stand confronted with man's great nuclear and interplanetary adventure and all the spiritual choices that are involved.

The first attempts at an organized lay apostolate were made in a static situation, which one might call a closed circuit. The word "hierarchy" was practically identical with Church, and meant the Church which thinks, administers and disposes; "priesthood" was a docile stream flowing through the valleys; "laity" meant to listen, to accept, and to obey. Having found a certain order and equilibrium, they all moved along in relative harmony, with no disturbing back-eddies or problems.

Nevertheless, the fact that laymen had shown a desire for an organized apostolate was the first symptom, recognized a hundred years ago, of their need for a specific responsibility, one which they alone could assume within the Church. "The laity is also the Church," was the title of a book by Archbishop Bazelaire of Chambéry. This appropriate and concise formula is an excellent expression of the goals toward which twenty years of questions and reflection have been gradually leading.

In view of all the words of theologians, priests and laymen in this area, our hope is to see the Council ask Catholics to confront their doubts with a source like Pius XII's encyclical on the Mystical Body, which they know so little and so poorly. We believe that the labor of reflection and meditation that is needed can find its true meaning and effective development only in the conviction that the Church is above all the living body of Christ. Juridical and functional distinctions are undoubtedly useful and even necessary, but they can be sterile and even become a stumbling block without a living current among members of the Church, an awareness of belonging to a single body, the desire to live with others in love in imitation of Christ's life, with each one free and responsible in the accomplishment of his role and the response to his vocation.

49

The Freedom of the Church in the Sovereignty of the State

The Church is catholic, that is to say, universal. But every Catholic is the citizen of a state, and every Catholic community part of a state. Once a Catholic community exists, we have the problem of Church-state relations, as well as the question of the relations between the freedom necessary to the Church (that is, its members) and the sovereignty of the state. No matter how crucial it may appear to the world today, this problem has existed since the first generation of Christians and cannot be ignored.

The dispute is always accompanied by disagreement, as much among citizens (Catholics or non-Catholics) who defend the sovereignty of the state, as among those (for the most part, Catholics) who defend the freedom of the Church.

Without exaggeration, we can say that this disagreement, especially among Catholics, has assumed an importance it never had before. In a way this is perfectly normal and understandable in a world divided between states which are totalitarian and those that are pluralistic, or which lean towards pluralism; in many countries Catholics face multiple and sometimes contradictory choices. The Church is engaged in an open struggle against that totalitarianism which deprives her of almost all freedom; but in the next instance she makes her peace with a certain totalitarianism which, though allowing her freedom and privileges, exercises its pressure in other directions, as well as against some of the regime's Catholics. Confronted with a variety of political orders, the Church finds herself in different conditions in each; everything depends on the degree to which she is able, more or less directly, to control and guide secular authority.

This state of affairs cannot last long without great damage to the freedom of the Church. Consequently, we hope that the Council will state precisely, in a clear declaration, under what conditions she considers herself free to exercise her full ministry to teach the gospel, offer various forms of worship, sponsor cultural activities, provide education —especially for the young, or maintain the initiatives which she takes in the realm of charity.

We hope that the Church will openly claim her right to freedom that is complete and without privileges, so that Catholics will feel obliged to keep her alive and active by means of their faith and a spirit of sacrifice and initiative. An example of Christian life in freedom without privileges is that of Catholics in the United States who, having achieved it over a long period, are now reaping its fruits.

We believe that many Italian Catholics share this desire for freedom without privilege, a situation all Catholics should strive for regardless of their political or social leanings. It corresponds to the Archbishop of Paderborn's ideas and opinions on the subject of Church-state relations, as expressed in his New Year's message of 1960, which a German publication called: "The End of the Constantine Era."

Spirit and Structures

Church-state relations have become difficult and complex precisely because of the evolution of social, political and economic structures.

The Catholics we meet every day, students, workers, government employees, office workers, generally accept the perpetual change of structures as a fact. They admit, even if with some confusion, that structural change involves both spiritual and technical factors. Without being Marxists or referring to Marxist doctrine, they are aware that scientific, technological and industrial progress means greater production. They are aware that greater production gives rise to problems of trade and distribution and to demands for new structures to replace those which are no longer adequate. They are more than ever aware that today the world is not composed exclusively of Christians (a realistic view inclines us to think that the number of non-Christians will increase faster than the number of Christians in the future) and that Christians have to cooperate with non-Christians in the technique of structural evolution. The Christian is distinguished from the non-Christian by the purpose and spirit of his work. Gradually, Christians are beginning to understand that it is by faithfully fulfilling his duties as a citizen, starting on the technical level, that the lay Christian breathes a soul into social structures— did not the early Christians breathe new spirit into the old pagan structures?—and shares in the *consecratio mundi* called for by Pius XII.

Other ideas are beginning to take shape among the Catholics with whom we collaborate in offices, schools, clubs, cultural societies, parishes and families: they are convinced that if social changes cannot be made gradually, that if they are held back too long, there will inevitably be violence; that social changes are bound to occur in spite of Catholic indifference. They do not believe that the Church is opposed to social changes as such, but to the violent form they often take; and that Christian truth, because eternal, cannot be linked to any one social system or civilization. All this has been confirmed over the past few years not only by theologians and sociologists but by the hierarchy itself. Many Catholics, particularly workers, complain that ever since the social changes which have been going on since the French revolution, the hierarchy has seemed to be saying "No." Although their attitude seems to have been based on spiritual reasons which were justifiable in themselves, their opposition blocked changes more than these reasons would require. Because of this phenomenon, Christian judgments and choices will not be unanimous. In countries where Christians have followed the dictates of their conscience and chosen to struggle, some with conservatives and others with liberals, both the spiritual and the temporal have benefited; there have been fewer jolts and more results worthy of both humanity and Christianity; the hierarchy has respected freedom of choice without labeling Catholics good, less good, or evil because of the parties they felt obliged to join.

Before so many choices, however uncertain, so many aspirations and expectations, we hope the Council will enlighten and guide us with explicit recognition of the effectiveness of Christian experience in freedom of political choice. At a moment when social evolution and all the contradiction it entails will surely be extraordinary, this would help to show that the Church of Christ, Mother of us all, is above partisan passions.

A Definite Tradition for Sincere Ecumenical Dialogue

It is generally understood that social structures evolve with the times, and that their contribution to the realization of "the common good" depends on the extent to which they fulfill the needs of successive generations; but no social structure can do this unless it is based on solid traditions.

Here the indictment of our country is unanimous. All classes of society join in denouncing the decadence of tradition and the intellectual indecency, as well as the political, financial and sensual shamelessness, of our times. Secular moralists expatiate on the subject in weekly magazines. Christian moralists, following traditional custom, are primarily concerned with the commandment against adultery, and wage a relentless battle against scandalous films, suggestive billboards, and the number of square inches of naked flesh on our beaches.

Everywhere one hears that nothing like this has ever been seen before. And the older people are not the only ones to shake their heads and turn nostalgically towards the past. The reason for all this becomes clear if one thinks of the increasing quantity of material goods at man's disposal, on the one hand, and the increased leisure, on the other. Sufficiently prepared for a life of work when goods were limited, contemporary man is unprepared for the abundance of material goods before his eyes and within his reach. Neither management nor labor is prepared; Christians, in spite of their Christianity and "Christian values," are no more prepared than non-Christians.

And we would not dare to claim that Christians, at least those in Italy, have been any less ambitious than non-Christians; our ambition has been closely linked to an unbridled activism, occasionally with apostolic goals.

It is sad to have to acknowledge all this, but it must be spoken of, and we must ask ourselves whether or not there is a complete lack of Christian tradition among Christians. The Sermon on the Mount insists on certain fundamental realities of Christian life; it reminds us that scandal and immorality are born in man's heart, that man has been placed on earth neither to despise material goods nor to allow himself to be dominated by them, but to obey God's Will; that this and love of neighbor are the only vocations of a Christian, and that they come before everything else. During the Last Supper, Christ explicitly stated that man can do nothing without Him and without Grace; we can only obey God's Will and love our neighbor by being united with Christ and responding to the appeals of grace.

We hope the Fathers of the Council will remind Catholics of these realities: failure to conform to them not only leads to disorder in our traditions, and in our modes of thought and action, but makes the difficult work of the apostolate unproductive.

The Apostasy of the Masses and the World of the Workers

It was Pius XII who first called the "apostasy of the workers" the "scandal of our times." We are not in a position to say whether the situation has improved since then or whether the scandal is any less. Cardinal Pizzardo, in his letter of July 3, 1959, to Cardinal Feltin, dealing with the question of priest-workers, wrote, in answer to the general alarm which the apostasy and dechristianization of the masses has caused: "It is difficult to consider men who have received the indelible mark of baptism as completely dechristianized." Holding on to this one fact out of many, he judged it "not essential to send priests to work in the environment of workers," and "to sacrifice the traditional concept of the priesthood to this end."[2] Yet, the problem of dechristianization was a problem of considerable concern at the last plenary of French Bishops in April, 1960. The Bishops made an urgent appeal to all Catholics to recognize the gravity of the situation and to unite in turning the tide.

We are not in a position to say to what degree the Italian situation corresponds to that in France. Those of us who have worked in large business concerns or who frequent borderline parishes composed mostly of workers, notice a slow, but constant detachment from all religious practice and Catholic truths. It is not necessarily a violent, polemical anti-clericalism but rather an indifference and unbelief, veiled by a smiling skepticism. Contacts between Catholics and non-Catholics in such an atmosphere are rare, outside of a common task on the technical level; this holds true as much for lay Catholics as it does for priests.

Saint Vincent de Paul societies are looked upon as little "clans" of

2 Cf. the letter of Cardinal Pizzardo, *Cross Currents*, Spring 1960.

kindly, well-intentioned people to whom one can refer a worker in need, confident that he will be given help regardless of his political affiliations, but with whom any spiritual or cultural exchange is impossible. The same can be said of the activist groups of the Catholic workers' association, the free syndicalists, and the Christian democrats. If spreading the Kingdom of God requires Christians to be the yeast in the dough, that is to say, a reality which works from within without being seen, one sadly wonders what sort of yeast is represented by these little groups which do not disappear but remain isolated and circumscribed by the very mass they should make rise.

Nevertheless, the situation is not hopeless. If we look at it closely, without being satisfied with appearances, we will see that the political struggle, the struggle for better working conditions, higher wages, and the purchase of a television set or a motor scooter, do not represent supreme satisfaction for the workers. Of course there is great enthusiasm on the day when a worker can buy his wife an electric iron, or when all the labor unions are in unanimous agreement on a common cause. But these are only moments. The daily routine quickly returns with the realization that the center of life is the family with its human warmth and work. One notices, too, that religion, with its feasts and preparations, still gives color to life, and people would really like to be certain that there is a Father who will invisibly accompany them to the harbor of peace, equality, and fraternity.

There exist the mass of men, and the aspirations, perhaps unconscious but profound, of the men who compose the mass. But there is no yeast truly capable of rising in the mass. Neither Catholic laymen nor priests constitute this yeast.

In Italy we have not had priest-workers. An Italian priest did, however, with his Bishop's approval, leave the parish where he had been loved and respected for ten years, to spend four years in a dockyard where he cut sheet-iron. With no danger to his faith or his morals, he was gradually able to enter into a cordial and sustained dialogue with his fellow workers. But when Cardinal Pizzardo's letter appeared he returned to his bishop and was assigned to another occupation.

We must also mention the experience of factory chaplains who belong to the O.N.A.R.M.O.[3] It is not surprising to find that they are looked upon suspiciously by workers who are convinced that they are on the "boss's side." After the Cardinal's letter these workers keep repeating: "You see, your church only wants priests to be officers and not just ordinary soldiers." They also asked, "If the atmosphere of the factory is so bad that priests are in danger of losing their souls, what about us, and you who are Catholics, how can you save your soul?" No mat-

---

3 *Opera Nazionale Asistenza Religiosa e Morale agli Operai*. Its seminary at Bologna forms factory chaplains and priests serving worker neighborhoods.

54

ter how logical and well thought out the replies were, they sounded empty to the men. One chaplain, who is completely free of all paternalism, and is genuinely aware of how hard the men in his factory worked, recently confessed: "They come to see me for recommendations, for a favor or to be well thought of by their boss because they think that priests have a great deal of power. But that is not why I went there nor why I want to meet them. This notion of paternalism is like a wall which has been rising between us for centuries. It is so detrimental to us that I constantly ask God to strike it down. Otherwise we will never get away from it."

Paternalism is a very serious matter, even though some Catholics smile and say that it is only a communist obsession. Yet the masses are devoted to the Christian idea that respect for justice and for the person is the first firm form of charity to man. They know that neither wealth nor social position gives any one the right to consider other men as inferiors to whom food and work are given as a favor. At any rate, it is very significant that the devotion of the masses to this idea is due to the efforts, sometimes violent, of non-Christians rather than Christians. Christians are still somewhat attached to a paternalistic mentality. This is evident in the conduct of Christian union members when they have to deal with representatives of management. Non-Christians are more frank and show greater freedom; Christian union members are often guilty of two contrary excesses: they either show an excessive respect, or adopt a provocative attitude characteristic of people who want to overcome their timidity. Both of these attitudes prove that they have not got beyond the paternalistic state of mind.

This servility does not date from yesterday. Nothing less than an encyclical (*Rerum Novarum*) and the words of a pope were needed to assure the majority of Christians, even workers, that it was perfectly legitimate for workers to organize and demand their rights from management. Pius XI, in *Quadragesimo Anno*, recalled the Catholic mentality and conditions which prevailed at the time of *Rerum Novarum:* "Instructions were published at a time when, completely subjected to liberalism, the governments of some nations did not encourage, not to say openly repressed, workers' associations. At the very time they recognized and protected such association in other classes of society, they shamefully denied the natural right of association to those who most needed protection. There was no dearth of Catholics to express grave doubts about the workers' attempts to organize, as though they had a lurking suspicion that they were socialistic or subversive."

After that, how can we not hope that the Fathers of the Council will urge Catholics to rid themselves completely of this mentality and persuade them to actively take up this struggle for justice which the French Bishops so vividly described in their statement on "the Class Struggle."

The French Bishops also asked Catholics not to abandon the struggle, even if it should arouse suspicion from other Catholics, who would consider them tarnished with socialism or subversion, since the efforts which Leo XIII approved and supported were similarly attacked.

Nevertheless, the "struggle for justice" is only one aspect of the problem. For a Catholic the essential task remains that of spreading the Gospel to the world of the working class which is waiting for it.

Contact with this world is difficult in itself. Yet, our recent experiences do seem to indicate some general directions and possibilities. We have in mind priests dedicated to poverty, living in working-class districts, free from all parochial duties and earning their livelihood as craftsmen—which would not run counter to ecclesiastical standards—or living from the gifts of the faithful; in this way they would be at the disposition of any one who would offer them friendship. Without having to proselytize, become sports fans or play cards, they would wait in prayer and meditation for occasions to meet men. They would have to be able to listen with limitless patience, without succumbing to the temptation to interrupt with theoretical discourses or declarations of principle, or to cathechize on the unions, politics or elections. We are convinced that the simple lives of such prophets would inspire laymen. We think that the Council should urge everyone to pray with confidence and perseverance that the Master send workers adapted to their times and for an abundant harvest. Christ himself said: "Pray to the Lord of the harvest to send workers for the harvest" (Matthew, 9, 38). Perhaps we have not taken Christ's words seriously enough: that is exactly why we should begin now.

translated by LÉON KING

John F. Bannan

The Council and the
American Catholic Experience

One's hopes for the Council are determined by one's conception of the best way in which to promote the Church's mission during the next few decades. Among the few predictions which can be made with confidence about this near future, two are outstanding: the first is that the Church will live as a minority in an awakening world population; the second is that within the Church, the laity will reach new levels of initiative. From each of these points of view, the American experience of the Church should be invaluable. The Church in America is at this moment a minority in a non-Catholic culture and among non-Catholic people with whom she has established an effective modus vivendi. Furthermore, American Catholic laymen not only enjoy an untroubled relation with their clergy, but they have an increasing general level of education. Each of these factors should serve well the exercise of responsibility to which they, like so many other Catholic laymen, frequently hear themselves called. Much then is to be hoped for from the American Catholic experience. Let us continue the dialogue with non-Catholics; let us reflect both upon it and upon the actual exercise of lay responsibility. As we do we shall help in an inimitable way to shape the Church's attitude toward those outside and to establish within, the psychological state adapted to the presence of lay initiative. We shall at the same time help clarify and advance the theological conceptions which will illuminate and orient the Church's life in our times.

Those who share this outlook may be tempted to hope that the Council will do *nothing*. Are not Roman decisions usually negative? Is there any more disheartening prospect for a promising tendency than a formal ecclesiastical pronouncement in its regard? The temptation to this position should, we feel, be resisted, and for reasons into which we will move shortly. First, let us face certain questions to which our glowing picture of American possibility must certainly give rise.

Can one really expect the dialogue with American non-Catholics to yield results applicable elsewhere? The American non-Catholic has a

John F. Bannan is one of the editors of Cross Currents *and teaches philosophy at Loyola University (Chicago). He is presently completing a book on Merleau-Ponty.*

high standard of living and of political liberty, and also a high level of education. In other areas of the world the "awakening" of populations is to conditions where there is very little of either. Without doubt, this disparity will qualify the applicability of the results of the American Catholic dialogue. But we American Catholics have had no choice but to treat non-Catholics as responsible human beings, to be addressed in terms of their capacity to freely accept or reject the Church. This is now habitual, and we can be sure that the "awakening" peoples will demand that such an attitude be taken toward them. Their freedom may strike us as something of a caricature, like the notion of maturity which belongs to the adolescent. But like that very notion, it will be an indispensable stage in a move to a more authentic freedom, and he will rightly demand that it be honored. If we are wise we shall respect it, and in fact make such respect a general style. Of course, once we do, our paternalism will be definitively modified.

But, it will be said, the American experience is the last place in which one would expect to find grounds for modifying Catholic paternalism. Is not the "untroubled relation" which American Catholics enjoy with their clergy, for all its freedom from classic anti-clericalism, thoroughly paternalistic? Unfortunately, *yes*. It must be conceded that for the American Catholic the reality of the Church and of her activities is identified very directly and explicitly with the controlling presence of priest and religious. It is difficult, however, to avoid the feeling that this fact is directly correlated with the very meager depth of participation in the Church by the layman. He touches its official life and it touches his day-to-day existence only occasionally and in highly limited ways. We suggest that this is because there is very little for him to do in the Church. He might have talent and energy to offer, but the apparatus for using his gift does not exist, and the attitude which takes joy in his initiative is yet to be established. *But it may be in sight:* this state of affairs is under heavy pressure, and there exists the possibility of resolving it in a way which would yield precious results. Here the position taken by the Council or, more properly, its *attitude,* may be decisive. Let us look more closely at the state of affairs and the pressures.

The increased level of education of Catholic laymen opens up for the Church as a whole, and for the first time in history, the opportunity to join the *experience* of the world with *reflection* upon that experience and with the establishment of policy according to that reflection. Surely the presence of the Church in the political, social and economic dimensions of the world can benefit from the variety of vehicles which the concrete experience of the political figure, the worker or organizer—*belonging* on these scenes as only a layman can—might provide. Certainly the Church's theology of marriage can benefit from the reflection of the men who are married . . . *and* of the married women. In the United States, as we have mentioned, more Catholics are getting more education than anywhere else. What can one among them do when he wishes to answer the summons to responsibility? He can write, and in this way attempt to sway "public opinion" in the Church. Beyond this, however, and particularly where situations call for close cooperation with the clergy, attitudes built up over centuries throw up impressive barriers. *Neither priest nor religious, on the one hand, nor laymen on the other yet know how to behave in a situation where the latter would have genuine initiative in a Church institution.* The necessary style of this coexistence has yet to be created.

This fact is now being driven home by a very significant development which has brought numerous laymen into a domain where exclusive prerogative has previously been exercised by clergy and religious. I speak of the recent developments in American Catholic Colleges and Universities, as a result of which the number of lay teachers and scholars in some is now far greater (at times ten to one) than the number from the order directing the institution. The laymen are the most completely educated among the Catholics and the most familiar with the call to responsibility. (The degree to which this situation is a microcosm of the state of the Church, and a testing-ground for the development of lay-clerical relations for the future has been given its due by no one, least of all those actually involved in it. Perhaps it is just as well, for the scene at the moment is rather depressing.) As might be expected, this "lay component" is now asking for a formal share in the determination of institutional policy. Reaction by the clerical and religious administrations varies from place to place, but it is a rare case in which it has not entered a stage which is purely and simply the stereotyped behavior of an established power in the face of the rising initiative of another group. It is an equally rare case that has really emerged from this behavior. "After all, it *is* our school." The laymen are not much more impressive. Much of their energy goes into uncertain groping for vehicles appropriate for their interests, and a good deal more into wondering whether their interests have any place whatever in a Church institution. "After all, it *is* their school." Past tradition is little help to either side in this question.

A moment ago we spoke the word which gives the key to the situation: *Power.* (It eases the tensions of the discussion to speak of *initiative,* or even better, *responsibility,* but the issue of power is always on the scene, and its presence should be acknowledged.) There is no responsibility without concomitant power; there can be no lay responsibility without corresponding lay power. We suspect that few of those who have called over the years for lay responsibility realized as they did that what they were asking for would make inevitable a modification in the manner in which power is exercised in the Church. When a group of lay persons asks for a *formal* share in the fashioning of policy in any Catholic institution, they are requesting one of the most difficult things in the realm of moral activity: that a group limit its own power. This step is especially difficult for clergy and religious who have had reason to see their power —even that which is the result of historical circumstance and *not* essentially related to the priestly and religious function—as an important factor in the divine plan for the salvation of men.

Fortunately, there are many areas of possible development of lay initiative which involve less directly the prerogatives historically wielded by the clergy and religious. Speaking recently of the Catholic attitude toward non-Catholics, Frederich Heer insisted upon the need for devising new ways of saying *yes* and *no,* ways genuinely respectful of their problems and persons. New styles of presence in the economic, political and social scenes must grow out of the concrete experience of those whose life in the Church is actually a life in these areas, so that there will be significant alternatives to mass action initiated by clerical directive. We feel, in fact, that the key to the exterior situation of the Church among non-Catholics lies in a special way in the solution of the problem of lay initiative within the Church. This, in its turn—at least in America—depends immeasurably upon the establishment of the appropriate psychological state in this infinitely complex organism. *This* is where the Council can be of the greatest importance, less perhaps by the literal content of its declarations than by the direction of its inclination. A widely expected move such as the renewed emphasis upon the role of the individual bishop would indicate a theme of decentralization valuable in the wider dissemination of responsibility. The equally anticipated revision of Canon Law to expand the legal status of the layman will help solidify his position. Such moves as these are our hope, for they will suggest to the clergy and religious that it may now be the time to begin seriously trusting the layman. They may remind the layman that he has rights, and, thus reassured, he may begin to trust himself. Should this come to pass, the future will be promising.

Daniel Callahan

The Council and the Catholic

*T*here is one thing immediately striking about the forthcoming Vatican Council: it has not been called to meet some great crisis in the life of the Church. Both the Council of Trent and the First Vatican Council were called so that the Church might equip itself better to meet dangers and threats both from without and from within. The emphasis, accordingly, in both was on shoring up walls which appeared to be cracking. The means employed toward this end, while not without great justification, were always in the direction of increased stringency of doctrine, restricted freedom of action and a sharpening of the differences between Catholicism and the other Christian churches.

The results of these two councils, while serving the needs of the Church at the time, have not in all instances been useful over the long run. Post-tridentine theology, as most theologians now judge, was far from perfect; in its desire to combat Protestantism it frequently managed also to constrict the development of the Church as well. The history of Catholic theology in the past four or five decades has been to balance and correct some of the excessive emphases of that theology. The Council of Trent, in particular, has come under close scrutiny; the work of Küng, Geiselmann, Jedin, Tavard, and Congar comes to mind immediately. The First Vatican Council suffered as much from its shortness as anything: it left up in the air a full theology of the Church. The setting for that Council was that of a Church threatened by Italian anti-clerical nationalism, the rise of the proletariat, the loss of temporal power by the Church and the dangers of secular rationalism.

It is clearly apparent how greatly the conditions under which Pope John XXIII called the forthcoming Council differ from those of the past two Councils. The Church is, in the material sense, strong and flourishing. The internal life of the Church is not today torn by strife or divided into warring factions; the current Biblical disputes, some unresolved matters of Church-state relations, the usual liberal-conservative divisions, are all *comparatively* peaceful. Finally, the Church faces no major danger to its existence from outside forces—Communism, while

Daniel Callahan is one of the editors of Commonweal *and was formerly a teaching fellow at the Harvard Divinity School. He is also one of the editors of the important collection of Catholic-Protestant discussion on major theological issues,* Christianity Divided *(Sheed and Ward).*

a threat, has not wrought appreciable international harm to the Church. In sum, the Church is comparatively strong and unified within and is meeting external threats in a moderately successful way. More important still is the fact that the past few decades have witnessed a remarkable flowering of Catholic theology, dogmatic, moral and pastoral. The Biblical revival, the liturgical movement, the catechetical movement, a revitalized missionary thrust, and a new look at dogmatic theology all suggest a great deal of life.

With these considerations in mind, I believe it can be said that this council has been called under very healthy circumstances: it was called for positive rather than negative purposes; it was called from a position of strength rather than a position of weakness; it was called to effect positive ends rather than to correct abuses or put enemies to rout.

I stress this point for an important reason. These are precisely the circumstances which ought to open up the *possibility* of genuine reforms, positive advances and help to establish an atmosphere of freedom from pressure conducive to progress. Above all, the circumstances of the Council make for an openness of mind and an optimism of outlook which should make it easier to do some productive work.

Avenues of Progress

Now the importance of the Council for the future of the Church will depend almost entirely upon whether these hopeful conditions are exploited. This could be done in two ways: by consolidating gains already made and by extending and deepening the life of the Church.

First, they can be exploited to consolidate and extend the gains that have already been made in the Church in recent decades. The most important gains seem to be as follows: the gradual development of a more viable notion of human freedom, both religious and political; the emergence of a revitalized—and theologically sounder—liturgical life; the emergence of a competent Biblical scholarship and a return to the Bible; a re-awakened interest in Christian unity; and a new understanding of the existential dimensions of Christian life. In each of these areas there has been considerable progress, considerable boldness and an unfolding of possibilities little conceived of by earlier generations.

Yet each of these important movements is very close to reaching the critical stage. For the most part, the great bulk of the progress has come from the work of individual scholars and minority groups within the Church. Though each has had the blessing and encouragement of the Magisterium, none has quite (with the exception, perhaps, of the liturgical movement) so proved itself that its work is beyond all danger of suffering a reversal—one need only recall the recent *monitum* on Biblical studies. Each of the movements has had opposition, each has had to struggle against critics within the Church who were hesitant, suspicious or hostile. So far these critics have managed to do little more than offer harassment; but the more advanced the movements become the more vociferous the critics are likely to become. Unless, that is, the Council can bless and establish beyond attack the work that has taken place recently.

This is particularly crucial in the area of the Church's recently awakened ecumenical interest. So far, the interest has been of a very general sort and good so far as it has gone. But it has, as yet, not gone far enough. The next stage of the Catholic ecumenical movement will be a far more difficult one than the first. The first stage concentrated on awakening interest in the problem of Christian unity and in urging charity, self-analysis and a sympathetic attempt to understand Reformation thought and its aftermath. The second stage, logically, should call for a close re-examination of the present teachings of the Church in the light of the need for Christian unity. It should call for a willingness to modify, where possible, those teachings and practices of the Church which are a hindrance to reunion. Along with this second step should go increased contacts between Catholic and non-Catholic scholars, clergy and laity—and constant *official* high-level discussions between members of the hierarchy and leaders of separated churches. The importance of the Council for the rapprochement of Christian Churches will lie in giving the present activities a formal stamp of approval and in making them an integral and important part of present Church life. That step taken, the more advanced steps can proceed from a firmly established base.

The *second* way in which the favorable conditions can be exploited lies in a deepening and extending of the life of the Church. Inevitably, this means that an attempt must be made to reform some practices within the Church, to point the way to further developments and to clarify some of the muddy issues which burden contemporary Catholic theology.

Now there has already been very much written about what the Council should take up and many opinions expressed about what probably seems most pressing. It would be somewhat idle here for me to offer simply one more list. Instead, I will offer a few suggestions written from the viewpoint of a Catholic layman concerned with Catholic ecumenicism. Some of the suggestions bear on what the Council might consider to make the lay Catholic a fuller participant in the quest for Christian unity. Most, however, bear on problems which seem to me to have direct relevance to the future of the Church's life and its relationship to other Christian churches.

Theological Problems

We may begin, first, with the most pressing theological problems:
1) *Authority and "free speech" in the Church.* It is quite clear to any-

63

one who has attempted to talk with Protestants and Orthodox about the Church, that the Catholic position on authority is by no means clear. There are two closely related aspects to the problem of authority: the authority of the Church and authority in the Church. The question of the authority of the Church has, in matters of faith and morals, been spelled out with some degree of clarity by previous councils (or so it seems to me). What has not, however, been spelled out very precisely is the authority of the Church in the social and political order. Here the problem is not so much one of making clear how far the Church's authority extends but, instead, that of defining precisely the limits of Church intervention.

The question of authority *in* the Church is far more complex. On the hierarchical level, the authority of the bishops needs to be more clearly defined as well as their position relative to the Pope. From all reports, this is already a matter which will be discussed.

But most pressing of all is the matter of "free speech" in the Church. The meaning of the phrase itself, and what it ought to mean in the context of the Church's right and duty to direct and instruct, is by no means clear. It is generally used in a positive sense to express the desire among many clergy and laity that they be given a more direct voice in the Church. In a more critical sense it expresses a desire for a greater latitude of opinion on controverted questions. For some years now this latter has been a problem which has greatly concerned many Catholics, not because of any particularly flagrant suppressions of individuals or ideas, but because it so often appears that those working on the frontiers of theological and social problems are liable to arbitrary silencing, hasty warnings from local ordinaries or superiors, and erratic suspicious opposition. The problem seems less to concern the action of the Pope than it does the authority—from the Curia down—at lower levels: too often the onus of proof of goodwill and theological rectitude is on the exploring individual; too frequently it is assumed that there is something dangerous in innovation, something dubious about experimentation. Too often no distinction is made between private opinion and the authoritative teaching of the Church.

In the ecumenical area, this attitude means a very inconsistent pattern of behavior on the part of ordinaries and superiors. In some dioceses (here I speak of America) bishops are eager to have priests and laymen take part in inter-faith programs, are willing to let local theologians sit down and discuss the deepest theological issues with non-Catholic theologians, and are very permissive in allowing laymen to work and talk with non-Catholics. But in many dioceses the opposite is true. In at least one of the largest archdioceses in America, the local clergy are always refused permission to engage in any kind of ecumenical dialogue, nor are theologians from outside the diocese allowed to accept invitations to take part in any kind of local discussion. This kind of inconsistency needs to be forestalled and some objective criteria established which transcend the patterns of particular dioceses. In general, one would hope to see the Church's ecumenical thrust so firmly established that the hesitant bishop would find himself clearly going against the current of the Church.

Important, too, is the need for establishing better means for the laity to make known their feelings and opinions to the hierarchy. For the most part, there is no formal way that the laity can do so now. This is a particularly bad—and potentially dangerous—situation in those countries which have a rapidly growing class of educated and informed laity. Somehow they must be given a more integral role in the life of the Church. I would include here also the necessity of the Church's finding some way to make this role extend as far as the magisterium itself; at least it ought to be possible for the laity's viewpoint to have some direct impact on the decisions of the magisterium and not, as now, for them to be solely passive. This is especially true in the ecumenical context because the laity is on the whole much closer, in their day-to-day contacts, with non-Catholics than is the clergy. They are in a particularly good position to know the kind of impact which the Church makes on the non-Catholic and to be able to appraise the points of agreement, the direction of aspirations, and the existence of points of friction.

It would, however, be misleading to mention authority and freedom in the Church without, at the same time, pointing out the existence of a dilemma. The dilemma is that between strengthening the Papacy and the Holy Office and that of increasing the autonomy of local ordinaries, superiors of orders—and even that of the individual priest and lay Catholic.

On the one hand, it is surely desirable that the Papacy be strengthened at least to the extent that the highest decisions of the Church will be accepted, implemented and applied throughout the Church universal. As matters stand now, it too frequently happens that the most healthful and promising steps taken by the Pope and the Holy Office are simply ignored on the local level. This has patently been the case in the decrees concerning the liturgical movement; innumerable bishops have simply done nothing whatever to implement these decrees and those priests and laymen who have used the authority of the decrees to press the matter have sometimes been handled very roughly. In recent years the Papacy has often been, in its social and political thinking, far in advance of the rest of the Church; too often this progressive thinking is not reflected and amplified on the local level. Taken together these facts would suggest the need for a more effective implementation of the directives and decisions of the Papacy.

On the other hand, there can be no doubt that a further strengthening of the Papacy could have the effect of diminishing local initiative and curtailing the kind of experimentation that can most effectively take place on the parish or diocesan level. Further strengthening would also inevitably have the effect of reducing still more the authority of the bishops. A Church in which individual bishops could not act without first consulting Rome would be both unwieldy and unhealthy. Still another major disadvantage would be the possible curtailment of free speech by the need of constantly deferring to Rome before opening one's mouth.

The main requirement, if there is to be such a thing as "free speech" in the Church, is that authoritative instructions, definitions and directives laid down in Rome be flexible enough to allow room for broad discussion and the possibility of effective criticism if the situation seems to require it. Free speech would simply not be possible if Rome always invoked its full power and always spelled itself out in absolute, inflexible terms. The very possibility of free speech demands that Rome allow as much room as possible for individual differences and leave as many controversies as possible open to continuing discussion. The climate necessary for the effective flourishing of free speech also requires a certain confidence on the part of Catholics that Rome is not watching their every move and is not prepared instantly to suppress and condemn.

The dilemma, then, seems to me a very real one and there appears to be only one effective way of getting out of it. That is, put in general terms, a Rome quick to commend and zealous in exercising leadership, and slow to condemn and to exercise its suppressive powers. It might be mentioned, in concluding this point, that the dilemma sketched concerning the power of the Papacy and the Holy Office has an obvious parallel on the diocesan and national level. To give the bishop greater freedom and autonomy could mean that the individual Catholic under his jurisdiction would have less freedom to avail himself of whatever progress Rome might initiate and encourage and less chance of having recourse to Rome for redress of injuries. Here again, one would want to see strength of leadership and slowness in applying restrictions.

2) *Religious toleration.* My second major point of theological concern is that there is a very definite need for the Church to be far more specific than it has been in the past concerning religious freedom. There can be little doubt that the Church has advanced very far since the nineteenth century in granting the non-Catholic the right to follow his conscience in his religious life. Here again, however, it is a question of advances made on a wide area by numerous theologians rather than in authoritative declarations by the magisterium. One can find among theologians today something very close to a consensus on the rights of non-Catholics; yet one can find very few Papal statements which could be said to show definitively that a major change has taken place in the Church's thinking. The result is that it often appears possible to defend totally incompatible positions with each side claiming the support of authority.

66

One obvious trouble, though, about pressing the Church for a more specific declaration on the rights of conscience is that the time may not yet be quite ripe for it. Even granting the great theological development which has taken place there is little to guarantee that this development is so well-established that it could, in direct confrontation with the opposition, gain its point on the highest level. This is, however, a problem that arises in almost every area which the Council is likely to consider: so much has happened so rapidly in recent decades that one can have no special assurance that any developments have taken solid root.

Yet, on the whole, one could hope that the Council would take up the question of toleration and religious freedom. The ramifications of some kind of positive declaration would be healthy for the inner life of the Church as well as offering reassurance to non-Catholics that the Church stands fully committed to human freedom. For the inner life of the Church it would create indirectly that bias in favor of freedom which often appears lacking.

3) *Reason and revelation.* My third point bears on the role and place of reason in religious thinking and in the development of theological systems. One of the constantly recurring problems in ecumenical encounter between Catholics and Protestants is the differing role each assigns to reason. For many Protestants, the traditional Catholic faith in the power of reason is a major stumbling block: an instance, it appears to them, of Catholicism's failure to appreciate the radicalness of Christ's Word and of its tendency to rely on man's autonomous power to appropriate God's truth.

The importance of this apparently great difference between Protestantism and Catholicism does not bear exclusively on the power of reason. Instead, it merely points up the general question of the power God has given to man to appropriate and forward His truth. For the one thing above all of which both Catholics and Protestants accuse each other is pride. The Protestant often seems to believe that the Catholic is guilty of pride in asserting that God has given to a Church composed of human beings the keys to the kingdom, that the Church is Christ extended on earth, that it is possible, in witnessing the Christian kerygma, for the Church to speak the truth without that truth being tainted by human sin and self-interest, that revelation is a completing and fulfilling of the perception of a truth which is open to man's unaided reason rather than a confounding of human speculations. The Catholic often believes that the Protestant is guilty of pride if he asserts that he can know the will of God without the help of the Church, in asserting that he can achieve salvation without any human authority to assist him, in asserting that the deposit of faith can be preserved—and immediately grasped—solely through the efforts of individual man.

There is some truth in each of these counter-beliefs; there is also considerable distortion. It is surely true that Catholics often appear to so

exalt reason that revelation seems to become superfluous, and that Protestants so exalt freedom that objective truth seems a minor concern. But
there is a considerable danger in putting the issues so baldly: both
Protestants and Catholics would hold that theirs is the only way of not
putting man in the place of God, of avoiding the great sin of pride; each
is well aware of the danger of pride.

The immediate difficulty with such a wide—and rather slippery—difference as the above cluster of attitudes suggest is that they are not directly amenable to Conciliar decision. What one could hope for, however, from the Council is some clear sign that, while reason is valid in
its own sphere, the Church is fully open to the prompting of the Holy
Spirit and that the Church forever stands open to the judgment of God.
In its need to exalt reason in the face of secular skepticism the Church
has often given the appearance that it was suffering just one more ra-
tionalist ideology to combat the ills of the age. In its need to exalt the
Church in the face of a destructive individualism and subjectivism the
Church has sometimes made it appear that it is a self-sufficient institution supplanting rather than serving God. Both impressions are erroneous but both impressions exist. The only way to counteract such impressions is to repeat again and again the proper relationship that holds
between Church and God, man and God, human power and divine
transcendence, human reason and human finitude.

But aside from statements and declarations about those relationships,
the most effective way to make clear the Church's conception of itself as
subject to the will of God is by its willingness to undertake self-analysis
and self-criticism, to reform and purify itself when the situation demands
it. To show, that is, that the Church is fully aware that it is, in some
areas, subject to the ravages of time.

Some Practical Steps

This brings me to the second set of themes which I hope the Council
will consider. These bear on some practical steps which the Church
might take in the direction of purification and renewal (and once again
I am limiting myself to those points which seem to have ecumenical
bearing).

1) *The reformation of seminary training.* One of the great handicaps
of the contemporary Church is that the ordinary seminary is almost
entirely cut off from the mainstream of ordinary life, both in its human
and in its intellectual currents. The typical seminarian has very little
contact even with his fellow Catholics (especially the laity). He has even
less contact with the intellectual and social movements of the day: the
movements whose air his parishioners breathe. The contents of his
courses are so heavily weighted toward theology and philosophy that the
result is almost inevitably a lack of awareness of the actual forces that

move his society: its political life, its literary activity, its social trends, its educational direction. His professors, while having more personal freedom to move out of the seminary in a physical sense, are hardly less cut off. The usual separation of the seminary and the university, of the training center and the place of speculation and research, are equally hard on professor and student. Doubtless, this separation has some advantages for the spiritual life in the sense that distractions are removed. On the whole, however, the result seems to have been a clergy who start their work under the great handicap of knowing too little about the world in which they and their parishioners live.

The result of this separation and consequent lack of knowledge is particularly bad in the Church's confrontation of secular humanism; the ordinary seminary course can show (at an antiseptic distance) what the evil is but it is hard-pressed to show how and why some of this evil may be traceable to our own shortcomings and failures. Indeed, few seminary courses are designed even to approach such a problem. Nor can it very well get at the dynamic sources of this secularism to show in what sense it may spring from a thwarted religious drive and a misunderstanding of the meaning of God and the Church.

This separation of seminary and people, training and speculation, is hardly less debilitating in ecumenical matters. It is simply not possible to understand the meaning of Protestantism or Orthodoxy without close and intimate contact with Protestants and Orthodox—Protestants and Orthodox as human beings rather than as devotees of erroneous doctrines. One might hope that means could be discovered which would make it possible for dialogue to develop on the seminary level—at that point in life when attitudes are in the process of formation. If, as everyone recognizes, Christian unity is a thing of the far, far distant future involving the work of men at all levels, than it seems absolutely essential that the aspirant priest be introduced immediately to the whole question and to the people who, together with him, may manage to bring it about.

2) *The deepening, furthering, and implementing of the liturgical movement.* It has often been said, and with great truth, that the present liturgical revival offers one of the best means of furthering Christian unity. For it is a movement which directly bears on the most important act of the Christian life: the act of worshipping God. A purification and renewal of an unceasing kind in this area cannot help but bear fruit in all areas of the Christian life. In particular, a greater participation by the laity in the Mass—the Mass as community worship—would help to break down an over-sharp distinction between laity and clergy in the Church, and make the doctrine of the Church as the Mystical Body of Christ deeper in its impact on Catholics and non-Catholics.

3) *The effective utilization of the laity.* While I have already touched upon this problem as a theological one, it is worth re-stressing as a prac-

tical problem as well. The need here is for far more effective means of employing the zealous layman in the Church: of improving lay understanding of the theology and life of the Church. More pointedly, a careful re-examination of the relationship of the parish to the Church universal is needed. The educated layman in particular increasingly finds that the ordinary parish lags so far behind the general developments in Church life to which he has been introduced in the college or university that there seems to be no place for him. In ecumenical matters, it is a source of distress to many laymen that all the work goes on at levels from which he is decisively excluded.

Perhaps the most important of all is the need to find ways of reducing the usual gap between the theological advances and popular piety. This is a gap which has always been present in the Church; it often takes generations for the Church universal to be influenced and changed by even the most firmly established developments. There is no simple solution to this problem; only a general climate of appreciation for, and openness to, innovation and change could do much to reduce the gap. A well-educated laity, however, would be a great help and would be a means of directly and rapidly introducing change into the lifestream of the Church—and of providing an immediate popular basis for any changes. This was hardly possible in the past when there was such a large gap between the intellectual level of clergy and laity; but this situation is changing rapidly and, if pressed, could mean a Church much quicker to respond at all levels to whatever new directions the Church might take. Moreover, as the Council of Florence showed, any movement toward Christian unity needs a firm, popular base.

In concluding this essay, I would like to call attention once more to the fact that the Council has been called under favorable historical conditions and springs from a desire to effect some positive ends. Every Catholic is grateful for the initiative and wisdom of Pope John XXIII in calling for a Council. The realization that the work of the Council will deal specifically with the inner life of the Church and only indirectly with Christian unity ought to dampen no one's enthusiasm—especially those non-Catholics who have felt that an examination of conscience on the part of Catholicism is a necessary step in any movement toward reunion. Equally hopeful, I believe, is the fact that there are so many new developments, new attitudes and new enthusiasms present in the contemporary Catholic Church. Few have come to anywhere near full fruition and there are still many obstacles standing in their way. But there is also a quite new and unique spirit of self-criticism and self-examination in the Church today, a spirit positive in its aim and lacking the overtones of bitterness that caused upheaval in the past. Surely Catholics and non-Catholics ought to find cause for rejoicing here—and cause for optimism.

What, finally, ought the Catholic be able to hope for from his separated brethren? Many things indeed. But I will mention only one. He ought to be able to hope that his own self-criticism will be noted by the non-Catholic, that his efforts to purify and enrich the Church will not be ignored. Doubtless, whatever is done will not be enough to satisfy all non-Catholics. But if it is kept in mind that self-criticism comes hard to Catholicism, other Christian churches may, for their part, be spurred to increase their own self-examination. For it has always been the great claim of Protestantism that it is open to radical evaluation and judgment of itself. It would surely be a great tragedy if the very painful Catholic efforts toward reformation and renewal are not matched by equally painful Protestant efforts.

Andrej Krasinski

Christians in a Socialist Society

Since all Catholics are invited to participate in the preparation for that great event, the next Council, a Polish contribution based on experience different from that of other Christian countries might be in order. At the start, it should be noted that this contribution has no pretensions to being official or even representative and will be somewhat outside the Council's main theme. In the contemporary world, however, it seems obviously impossible to deal with problems of the relationship between Catholics and other Christian confessions without also coming to grips with their relations to all others, especially non-believers and those who are indifferent. It is equally impossible to handle these problems without seeing the new problems faced by Catholics in countries where Christianity, though still alive and strong, cannot identify itself—as it once could—with the dominant culture.

This does not mean that ecumenical questions, in the narrow sense of the word, are of no interest to Polish Catholicism. On the contrary, a great effort at information and clarification has been undertaken by the Catholic press and various study groups. Nonetheless, in Poland, where there are few Christians of other denominations, interest in the Council would be mainly a matter of this broader interpretation embracing all the problems of the relations of Christians and non-Christians, including atheists.

With few exceptions, in all modern societies Catholics are called upon in the name of the common good to cooperate closely with non-believers. They may accept or refuse cooperation, depending on the circumstances, without causing serious consequences or problems of conscience. In a country like Poland, however, the issue is more important and complex. It is not just a question of collaboration on occasion but of becoming involved in the life of a new society, in the construction of a society animated by an ideology opposed to Christianity. There would seem to be no way out of the dilemma if it were not possible to distinguish between the real society and its proclaimed ideology. This is not merely a theoretical distinction, but one involving an essential difference in perspective. For most people living in capitalist countries, socialism is an abstract program evaluated from theoretical and ideo-

Andrej Krasinski is a Polish poet and essayist. He is one of the editors of WIEZ *and recently edited a volume of selected writings of Mounier.*

logical points of view. For Polish Catholics, however, socialism is an actual fact and has to be lived with; if they wish to change it in any significant way, they must take into account its concrete existence.

In such a context one finds the possibilities of cooperation with others, but this means some form of involvement in socialist society. It seems futile to believe that this choice can be avoided by making a sharp distinction between a social commitment directed towards the common good and relations with the State and its power. Under existing, not imaginary, socialist conditions, wherever a person is committed to serving the common good, he runs into the State's organizational and regulatory activities. Whether we like it or not, the State's centralized direction of social forces has resulted in extremely rapid economic growth and unprecedented social advancement. We are well aware of the abuses of centralized control but they do not change this statement's essential truth.

Faced with this fact, Catholics have adopted different attitudes, which may be classified according to certain general characteristics. First of all there is the attitude which tends to reduce to a minimum all contact and ties with the life of the new society. It is a temptation to keep intact, in spite of changes that have taken place, the old model of relations between the individual and society. It goes without saying that this can be done only by voluntarily condemning oneself to life on the margin of society, psychologically as well as materially. It is pointless to emphasize the dangers of such a position for the survival and spread of Christianity in a socialist world. This attitude, however, was very widespread especially during the years just after the revolution.

On the other hand, from the beginning of the new experiment, the mass of Catholics adopted a different attitude. Without posing too many problems for themselves and, at the same time, seeing no other way out, this group became involved in the construction of socialist society. Certainly, theirs was not commitment in the most exacting sense of the word—that is, fully conscious choice—but it would also be wrong to pretend that it was merely passive adaptation. This Catholic mass was pulled along by the flow of technological and structural change; it benefited from extremely rapid social progress. It should be remembered that the process of urbanization and industrialization lasted about a century and a half in western Europe, while in many areas and localities of Poland the overthrow of traditional structures and patterns of thought was accomplished in less than fifteen years. Catholics constitute the majority of the enormous mass of people flowing into cities; but if this group remains Catholic, it is due to the influence of tradition and personal needs. Unfortunately, however, because of the way it is too frequently presented, Catholicism appears to the urban masses as strictly tied to the old ways of living; that is, it is something which has

73

little to do with daily life. Thus, between the life of faith and social and civic life, a dangerous break appears and may very well widen.

In face of this danger, some have tried to fill the gap through political action, constituting a new form of "political Catholicism" whose results have been deplorable. This approach has been rightly critical of the effects of a dangerous amalgamation of religious and political elements in bourgeois societies, but at the same time, it has not been able to avoid similar and even more serious confusion. Augmented by a superficial ideological syncretism in an attempt to adapt itself to certain marxist themes, this attitude carries with it all the perils and traps of the *progressiste* experience after World War II. At the same time, it also embodies the famous slogan "politics first," but this time in the context of a socialist society.

There are not only undeniable doctrinal dangers in such a course but it is also quite incapable of filling the gap under discussion. It seems clear that it is impossible to reconcile man with this new civilization by political action as such. This is not a question of recommending or defending a so-called a-political attitude which has so often hidden quite definite political positions. On the contrary, under Polish conditions political choice is more necessary than ever; but it cannot be motivated by a taste for the game of politics or the attraction of power. It must be dictated by a need to give witness and clarify the attitudes of Christians in relation to social and political life. However, political activity, especially within the framework of political institutions in socialist society, runs the risk of having contradictory effects: that is, making it seem that the essential task is merely one of borrowing phraseology and practicing political conformity. In fact, this is often a cloak for traditional attitudes and models of behavior which are completely anachronistic in relation to the new conditions of social life.

The real problems lie elsewhere. Certainly, an *a priori* political position can enclose people in an attitude of isolation and total refusal. However, changing civilization and time itself make this attitude almost impossible. Today the structures of socialist society are already firmly in place and great social changes are incontestably irreversible. It is foolish to continue political debate over the advantages and inadequacies of socialism as such. What is important is the man of the future in this new society and the concrete character of the culture that is arising within a framework of socialist institutions.

It is completely false to believe that this culture is being shaped by the influence of marxism alone. If one has only a general knowledge of Polish reality, one knows that ideology and theory have but limited influence. On the other hand, one cannot overestimate the changes in consciousness and attitudes which are brought about by the influence of the actual transformations in civilization advocated and achieved by the marxists. Fifteen years' experience has already shown a consider-

74

able gap (above all in the cultural field) between intentions and pro-grams, on the one hand, and the results obtained, on the other.

The culture one sees developing is far from being homogeneous; it is taking shape very slowly and, in part, spontaneously as the result of different and sometimes even contradictory forces. In this melting pot where the model of a future socialist culture is being formed, it seems there is room for diverse influences as long as they are adapted to the framework of life and, above all, capable of increasing man's creative forces within the surrounding conditions.

Abstracting from real difficulties and conflicts, often very serious, and attempting to grasp the long-range historic perspective of Christianity in the socialist world, we see that the possibilities of a flourish-ing faith depend above all on an ability to advance these civilizing tendencies.

This implies an attitude receptive to cooperation and commitment which is not preoccupied with criticizing or changing existing institu-tions. It means introducing a spiritual ferment, and firmly establishing Christian values in the peoples' conscience which would be capable of guiding not only their individual behavior but also their activities and relations to society.

Above all, it is the mass of laymen who are responsible for these tasks. It is obviously neither the Church as an institution nor the clergy that are called upon to perform this task. If in each society the character of the layman's commitment is essentially different from the priest's, the difference becomes more distinct and clear-cut when the State is not neutral, when it is inspired by an ideology contrary to Christianity. Relations between laymen and clergy then assume special importance, while traditional forms of these relations are no longer satisfactory. Rap-id changes of civilization have modified the priest's social status. If the village pastor, precisely because of his religious role, was integrated into the rural community, in industrial and urban civilization his sacerdotal functions tend to place him on the margin of society. It is quite clear that this new situation demands that the priest's faith express itself in something more than his religious and moral behavior. If laymen are to be helped by the priest, he must have a deep understanding of prob-lems of social life and the needs of man; he must also be sensitive to the fundamental values recognized by the society, even those which do not stem from Christianity but still deserve recognition because of their content. Thus new problems are posed for the training of priests.

In addition, new problems are also created in regard to the training of laymen. The traditional model for this formation contains a two-fold danger. First of all, it runs the risk of enclosing Christians within an individualistic attitude, linked to forms of sentimentality and customs arising out of traditional institutions. In this situation it is difficult to rediscover the ties between faith and social life with its new demands.

Secondly, and more generally, for a society in the process of rapid transformation, this traditional and individualistic attitude acts as a brake or an obstacle to the necessary socio-cultural adaptation.

In dealing with problems faced by Catholics in a Socialist country, it may seem incomprehensible to Western readers that no mention has been made of the difficulties and conflicts encountered in the course of that experience. If the many thorny issues which have arisen during the past years have not been raised, it is simply because in a situation where two opposing attitudes confront one another, each must begin by examining its own tasks and responsibilities. If both sides are worried only about heaping blame for all defects on the other, if each is preoccupied in demonstrating only what the other should have done or thought, such a confrontation will have little chance of being fruitful. The condition for any effective dialogue is, in the first place, to understand the other and then see clearly whatever is contingent, hence variable in one's own attitude, and what should remain unchanged. Under the circumstances, understanding the other means abandoning a militant and blind anti-communism so common among Christians. For too long a time, this stand-pat position has hidden from Westerners the complex reality of an entire world which is growing and developing according to its own logic.

Since we are present at the birth of a new civilization of work, we must do everything possible to prevent Christianity from being tied in the eyes of the people to European forms of civilization, bourgeois forms of society. The experiences undergone by Poland have favored and accelerated the disentangling of Christianity from these contingent, historic links. But this process cannot be carried out only by Christians living in socialist countries. In order for it to be valid and for the preservation of Christian unity it must be understood and supported by the whole Catholic world. At this decisive moment, when the idea of Catholic universality is taking on its full meaning, when considerable effort has already been made in order that the Christian message spring up in the very heart of the new societies which are awakening and beginning an independent life, a similar effort is urgently needed in the socialist world.

translated by MARTHA and BOB FAULHABER

Jose-Luis Aranguren

The Council in a Secular Society

*T*he next Council is going to assemble at a critical moment in the history of the Church. It is a moment when, in the eyes of the world, it has taken on an importance that is more "political" and "social"—in the widest sense of these words—than "religious" or "spiritual."

Let us not deceive ourselves. Whether we are Catholics or not, let us try to see things as they really are, and not as we wish they were. For a long time now the Church has stopped being the essential pillar of culture. There was a time of "Christian civilization," but we have moved beyond it. What I mean by this is not only that the Church as such, or the Church as institution, has stopped being the subject of our civilization; all that is well understood and has been the case for centuries. Nevertheless, in the absence of the Church, Catholic philosophers, theologians, poets, novelists, essayists—Claudel and Mauriac, Scheler and Guardini, Maritain, Blondel and Mounier, Chesterton and Graham Greene, among many others—have for a quarter of a century and more figured among the great creators of an epoch. In spite of everything, certain symptoms seem to announce, along with the loss of intellectual vitality by Catholics, the return of Catholicism to what is, after all, its "modern" situation—that of the 18th and 19th centuries—that of a peripheral reality, marginal or antagonistic.

The men of today have discovered, after having experienced it, that *it is possible to live in contingency,* that one can *be quite comfortable* there and *become quite accustomed* to it. This general tendency, which is most notable among the young, to a renunciation of transcendence, to live without hope, without *inquietude,* and without sectarianism, in order to concentrate one's whole life in *this world,* is, I believe, an important new element for our time, heavy with consequences from a religious point of view. The next Council is going to take place in a period of secularization, in a time of positivist realism, of open battle for concrete interests, and of "materialism" (eastern or western). Such will be the cultural-historical context of the Council.

In this we discover the primary objective of the Council: to bear an

José-Luis Aranguren is professor of ethics at the University of Madrid, and the author of Catolicismo y Protestantismo como Formas de Existencia, *which has been translated from its original Spanish, and will soon appear in English.*

unimpeachable witness to the sacred in a world more and more turned toward the here-and-now, to serve the cause of authentic religion. It is clear, therefore, that it is not so much a matter of one or another theme to be taken up by the Council, as the position it will take in order to proceed to its end, and the tone that will be adopted.

The secularization of our age is a reality which must be taken into consideration, and which should serve as a point of departure. It is important that this witness of the sacred be at least accessible to a world which is progressively separating itself from religion. The excessive distance between this world and the ecclesiastical mentality can only be crossed if the Church boldly has recourse to *laymen*. The next Council ought to proceed to the advancement of the layman's world. This should not be done simply out of a spirit of religious justice, but also because of overriding necessity in the domain of the spiritual. Simply as an ecclesiastical authority, the Church is stumbling—and will stumble more and more—over almost insurmountable difficulties in trying to put itself into the mentality and sensibility of today, in order to speak to our time and hear what it says. A system of intermediary groups is needed whose function would be to provide the data on temporal reality and make the Gospel message both comprehensible and contemporary. This can be established only with the help of laymen. The Catholic who lives in the world ought to acquire, even in his style of life, a more exemplary efficacy; he might adopt, for example, a conception of asceticism as the Christian acceptance of the agonies that life brings. Here is an area in which a concrete theology of perfection could do useful work.

We said before that the days were over when the Church, as institution, was the creator of culture; they are finished and will not return. That is why the legitimate aspiration which wants Christianity to be, or become again creative, should find its application in the secular world. In this way the freedom of the Catholic lay world presents itself as an indispensable condition of the vitality of the Church. The latter should profit from the adaptability of a dynamic and enterprising secular world which is capable—without committing the Church—of discovering and exploring new avenues for Catholicism.

This liberty, which is creative of spirituality under one of its aspects, ought at the same time to provide a needed self-criticism. In the religious system today, criticism within the Church corresponds—quite modestly, it is true, for the times are different—to the role the prophets played for our forefathers.

We began by considering Christianity as a testimony to the sacred, which seems all but lost in the world which grows more secular each day; in such a context it appears unbelievably anachronistic to hold on either to Protestant anti-Rome attitudes, or to anti-Protestant Counter-

Reformation positions. When the problem which we must face today is *de-Christianization,* how can we waste our time in highly un-Christian polemics among Christians?

The second great task of the Council, therefore, is a radical change of attitude on the part of Catholics to their schismatic brothers. Let us emphasize that it is not a question of minimizing differences nor of advocating any kind of dogmatic indifference. The differences are there and we would only be deceiving ourselves if we closed our eyes to them. Even more, we may say—following Oscar Cullmann—that these differences are actually incompatible, and because of them union, humanly speaking, is impossible. For example, the Catholic Church would cease to be itself if it consented to a union which did not consist in a return to its midst of those who were separated from her, since she considers herself to be, from the dogmatic point of view, the true and only Church. But let us leave the level of dogma for a moment and ask ourselves: if we really desire union, would it not be better facilitated if this quality of being the true and only Church were recognized spontaneously by dissidents? Why not let it become apparent from reality itself, no longer claimed by empty words but by facts, and stop proclaiming for ourselves—at the risk of passing for pharisees imbued with their own perfection—exclusive rights to our Church?

We mentioned earlier that Catholic laymen should be pioneers and explorers within the Church. This role, carried to the point of heresy, and unhappily, beyond it—but *oportet haereses esse*—has been conscientiously assumed by our Protestant brothers. I shall cite only one example: without Protestant biblical criticism, would the positive work of today's Catholic theology have been possible? "Free examination" has gone too far, but, humanly speaking, it is thanks to it that Catholic theology, without being stained with heresy, because others had previously paid that price, has attained levels which would hardly have been accessible without this paradoxical aid.

Indeed, as one can see, the task of the Council, rather than to deal with questions that have already been determined, is to lead Catholics to a revision of their position in regard to Protestants. Christian "fraternity" must not be limited to adding a few words to our ecumenical vocabulary; let it be a reality lived by each of us.

Even after one concedes the importance of theological disputes, it seems, nevertheless, that the most serious obstacles, encountered even by those Protestants most disposed to look towards the Church, are not simply on the dogmatic level, but might rather be called Roman "centralism" or "papalism." It all might be summed up as the sociological aspects of the Catholic world, that is, our scandalously anti-social way of living our religion, the superstitious aspect of a certain kind of popular piety, the Index and the way it is handled, etc. This kind of thing is also the principal stumbling block for many non-Christians who want to enter the Church.

That is why the attempt to purify the Church should be the third great task of the Council. As we have said, this requires an effort in the moral area. From one sociological point of view, an effort is needed to purify certain widespread methods which are only superficially "modern"—the misuse of publicity-oriented propaganda for sacred things—in order to adapt the message of the Gospel to the world. I said at the outset that people are looking to the Council for something more in the political order than in the spiritual. What I meant was that what people especially expect from it is either a firm commitment of the Vatican to the western bloc, or, on the contrary, if not a complete break, at least a relative withdrawal. One tends thus to give a political interpretation to the Council. Nevertheless, in the face of these expectations, the Council should show its firmness in refusing to play any political game whatsoever.

The Church knows that nothing can prevail against her. Why does it not rest peaceably in this conviction? The political attempt to utilize ecclesiastical power is a response to a lack of faith. While constantly preaching, in season and out of season, the duty of social justice, the Church ought to detach itself from any special class or specific bloc. The Church should not continue to be the Church of the bourgeoisie, nor try to be, in any exclusive sense, the Church of the proletariat. The Church can be neither western nor eastern, nor can she forget the new neutral nations which are emerging before our eyes. The Church must simply be Catholic, that is, universal.

It frequently happens that the Church denounces—or in order to obtain the political support of the Church, others denounce—marxist materialism, against which, we are told, one must take sides. This is true. But apart from the theoretical materialism of Marxism, there is also the practical materialism of the Welfare State. (It might even be said that in a certain degree the latter is more materialistic than the Communist state, since the citizen of a Communist country is called upon to sacrifice his egoism, while the perfect consumer is drawn by the very logic of the economy to develop and satisfy that materialistic egoism which is the real motor of economic life, and even of all life in the affluent society.) Would it not be a proof of anachronistic rationalism if if we took into consideration only *what was said* and did not look at *what was done?* The Church ought to commit itself boldly at the next Council to the path of moral, sociological and political purification. But let me be properly understood: political disengagement of the Church as such neither can nor ought to entail a lack of interest in politics. On the contrary, it should result in the free choice of Catholics in the domain of politics, choices taken on their personal responsibility. The theme of the freedom of the world of the layman, which we mentioned earlier, appears again at this point.

If numerous non-Catholics are interested in the Council because of what it can represent politically, there are also many Catholics, full of a naive freshness, who expect one or several miracles from it: peace, complete social justice, the liberation of nations and oppressed individuals. . . . For ourselves, more modestly, we hope it will represent a genuine step forward in the three areas that we have cited: the purification of the Church, the development of the Catholic layman to adulthood, and the establishment of a real fraternity between Catholics and other Christians. And through these three tasks, and as their crown, may the Council be able to offer to the "secularists" of today an authentic and total testimony, without equivocation, of the religion of Christ.

translated by JOSEPH E. CUNNEEN

H. A. Reinhold

The Expectations of the Faithful

When the Second Vatican Council was first announced by Pope John XXIII at St. Paul's Basilica in 1959, on the Feast of St. Paul's conversion, all of us looked up with great hope. There was the sound of the heart in the voice of the Holy Father; he seemed to be expressing the longing of all Christians for reunion. He emphasized that the Council should pave the way for further efforts and negotiations to make the Church of Christ one again.

In the meantime a great deal of retraction has been suggested by other official voices. There has been considerable work done by various preparatory commissions, an accumulation of studies made in good faith and in great hope, but the expectations of the faithful seem already to have met with a certain disappointment. It is impossible, however, to have an informed opinion as to much of what is going on; for example, the important commission of faith and doctrine, under the leadership of the Cardinals of the Holy Office, is under two oaths of secrecy, which are very well kept. The dynamics of negotiation is going on all the time, and it is important to remember that the Council itself will be guided in some degree by the Holy Spirit, but one cannot help feel that there is considerable resistance within the ecclesiastical structure to the possibility that the Council should be anything more than a routine affair.

It may well be that the publicity mechanism obscures more profound stirrings, but are those attending the Council willing to face the prospect of a totalitarian future for our planet? This could indeed come about, not only through the victory of Communism, but through an excessively negative reaction by non-Communist nations, or perhaps in some other form. We have only to recall the America of the '30s and compare it with the atmosphere of America today to see how much we have been restricted in our freedom. The Church must be concerned with this loss of freedom, and not simply in Communist-dominated nations. Economic privilege and the virus of racism already restrict the proclamation of its message in the "free world." Are we ready to consider the possibility of a more open hostility in which our institutions and most of our visible

As the columnist H. A. R. of ORATRE FRATRES *(now* WORSHIP*), Father Reinhold spent many years helping to develop the liturgical revival. He is also the author of* BRINGING THE MASS TO THE PEOPLE *(Helicon),* THE DYNAMICS OF LITURGY *(Macmillan), and* SOUL OF FIRE *(Meridian).*

props might be destroyed or taken away from us? Would we be prepared, intellectually, spiritually, and morally? Our plans for the future must include such a possibility; we have no right to leave such things to God's providence.

Of course, detailed legislation to bring the Church up to date is important. But is it important to give greater consideration to how—or whether—the Church might be so renewed and remolded that it would be a receptacle which autonomous churches could join by making a profession of faith in its essential doctrines? Is it merely a romantic notion to talk seriously of decentralizing the Church? In the light of the apostolic truth which the Church has preserved, is it necessary to insist constantly that the existing Roman Catholic Church is *the* Church? Far from constituting an invitation for churches with equal traditions, like the Orthodox, this approach suggests the parallel of the present "negotiations" between Russia and America, a dialogue of the deaf.

There are many noble Christian figures outside Rome who are showing increased appreciation of the deep spirituality of Catholicism, and who are trying to instill this awareness among their own groups. It is hard to explain to them, however, why this Church, which they have grown increasingly to love, at times seems wedded to the trappings of empire and the badges of rank. The effort to make an increased use of the language of the people in the liturgy of the Church has, understandably, been followed with sympathy by many of our separated brothers; here again, official opposition is often understood by them as an instinctive reaction to keep the Church exactly as it now is.

The larger question, however, is whether the survival of the Church really means that all other churches must go down on their knees and beg for admission. If Protestants and Orthodox are expected to look at the Primacy of the Holy Father in its present form and say to themselves: "It has survived the storms of 1059 and 1517; the Church must have a divine energy in itself"—if we expect the Protestants to do this, and the Orthodox, are we also willing to say that if the Orthodox Church has lasted nine hundred years and continually produced saints, and if Protestantism has revived with new spiritual energies after the disintegration of the last century, we must beat our breasts repentantly and recognize the hand of God in what is taking place? Our question today should not be posed in terms of the right church and the wrong church, but rather: how can we cooperate with the plan of Divine Providence for these units of Christianity that obviously bear within them the energies of the Holy Spirit and produce holy lay people and clergy?

Nobody doubts the right of the Church to regard itself as the only remnant of true believers, and to formulate its faith in dogmas like the Immaculate Conception and the Assumption of Our Lady. And if that is the wish of the majority of the bishops, and the desire of the Catholic faithful, the individual Catholic has to bow his head and accept these dogmas as he accepts the dogmas of Christ's divine and human natures, the all-saving worth of His sacrifice on the Cross, and the Real Presence under the species of bread and wine. But is there not a difference in rank between these teachings? If it is true that the East believes the same things that we do, but prefers not to formulate them in hard-and-fast dogmatic propositions, can we not accept our separate brothers without humiliating them? If Protestants are willing to retrace their steps and discover where they lost something substantial in the 16th and 18th centuries, can we not be magnanimous, allow them to gather up their catholic remnants, and show us a church that is spiritual, anchored in the fundamental belief in the Son of God, our Redeemer?

The second question, "What are the principal themes which the Council should take up?" is really too broad. It suggests possibilities in widely different categories, and I would not wish to suggest that all the points I might raise are of equal importance. In all its discussions, the Council should try to keep in mind the whole of mankind, not simply the wealthy nations of the "Christian West." In the light of the growing industrialization of the world, and the needs of the underdeveloped countries, is it not time for greater emphasis of a more communitarian view of economics? We must be honest enough to recognize that *Rerum Novarum,* admirable as it was, came too late to prevent "the scandal of the 19th century"—the loss of the working classes to the Church. Despite the many values in *Mater et Magistra,* it will prove inadequate to our revolutionary age unless it is followed up with bold initiatives and concrete action. It is extremely naive to see the Council primarily in political terms, but it is hard to guard against political appropriations of religious affirmations. What a tragedy it will be if we let Communism seem to be the only alternative to a "free" economy. Let us keep in mind that our great adversary is the practical materialism of the whole world, not simply one of its crystallizations in Communism. It is sobering to recognize that Christian adherents of all faiths are in the minority, and do not make a great impression on the majority of the world. Do even the vital Christian communions of Catholics and Protestants in France, Belgium, Holland, Germany, and the United States really give a Christian flavor—not simply denominationally correct, but according to the model of Christ—to their public lives? We might well ask to what degree the acquisitive bias of the economies of these countries has obscured the potentialities of Christian witness.

The frightening international situation underlines the need to formulate a new approach to war. Can we learn to replace the categories which were made in the days when man slaughtered man with his sword or bow and arrow? One of the conditions for the traditional Catholic teaching on a just war was a reasonable hope of success; this possibility has today been eliminated, for there can be no victor in a war fought with atomic weapons. Whether a new war would be as complete in its destruction as some have stated, or whether such predictions have been exaggerated, makes no difference if we are to take seriously the notion of the responsibility of the individual Christian. On what basis can we ask him to be convinced that war will remedy anything any more? World War I may be considered to have gotten rid of German imperialism; World War II got rid of Hitler. In order to get rid of Khrushchev, we would have to get rid of our own government, our own people, and the people of the world.

As far as internal problems in the Church are concerned, one of the most frequent suggestions has been for greater decentralization. It is hard to see how this can be done, as things now stand. A balance has been achieved between the power of the center and that of the individual diocese. There would be no check on bishops, if Rome were powerless; there would be no check on Rome, if bishops had no power. The several alternatives, which hardly seem imminent, would involve a thorough overhauling of the administrative structure of the Church. Those who talk glibly about "democratization" should realize that this is precisely the kind of problem which cannot be solved by speculative legislation or *a priori* sleight of hand. We might learn a good deal from the patriarchal Eastern Churches, which manage to preserve both a centralizing administration and the divine commission of both bishops and priests. A related concern has led some to urge the re-establishment of deacons in the Church, whether taken from lay people or from those who do not want to go on to the full priesthood.

In keeping with the universalist requirements of our times, it is often pointed out that the position of St. Thomas Aquinas as the unique teacher of the Church has in practice impeded the develoment of other schools of thought, and may unnecessarily delay the Christian use of various non-western philosophies. While St. Thomas is the clearest and safest interpreter of fundamental Catholic theology, this does not mean that he covers all the ground which Catholic thinkers, in following out the implications of the Incarnation, must include.

A similar sense of openness to the ongoing character of the Christian enterprise might well be useful in any conciliar discussion of the revision of seminary education. Future priests should be helped to gain a sympathetic awareness of the present and its problems, and competent laymen should be fully utilized in various areas of instruction. It might help to limit the time of complete seclusion from the world to the last four years in the seminary; college years could be spent in Catholic colleges. At present a very high percentage of vocations seems to come from a self-enclosed sociological ghetto. Have we done all that we might to make sure that future priests are attracted from as widely varied areas of Catholicism as possible?

The problems of decentralization and seminary training, however important, may yet be thought of as subordinate to the issue of liturgical revival; a reform and simplification of divine services is long overdue. The ancient liturgy is deserving of respect, but pride in our lineage is less important in this area than recapturing a spirit of youth and doing everything possible to make the inner meaning of the liturgy more available to the spiritually hungry masses of our day. The penitential discipline of the Church might also be examined from the same point of view. It needs refocusing and re-orientation. In many places the confessional has become an absolution-machine. Homiletics can be taught more seriously, and the new spirit of biblical homiletics should be given strong encouragement. Scripture services and bible vigils, which have been tried out in France and Belgium—and to a lesser extent, in the United States—deserve to be imitated in the whole Church. Another suggestion worthy of consideration is the distribution of communion under both species on certain occasions. This practice would appear to be feasible at retreats and other occasions when the congregations are small enough so that the service will be dignified.

An effort at clarification would be welcome in regard to the doctrine of purgatory. The Church has never defined purgatory as a place of fire. It should be taught as a state of purification in the most spiritual sense, without the gory detail that is now being preached and read in so many prayer books. The Council of Trent was very wise to guarantee only the fact that a purgatory exists and that we can help the souls in purgatory. That is all that was ever said on the basis of the infallibility of the Church.

Freedom in liturgical development from nation to nation would be a great encouragement to the new nations that are entering the Church in Africa and Asia. We have today enough scholars in Europe and America to take care of the historical and pastoral side of the needed liturgical reform, but it will seriously impede the gain that might be expected from this movement in the lives of the faithful if we remain Latin-speaking, at least in those parts of the Mass which require the participation and understanding of the people. It would also be unfortunate if an exaggerated insistence on Latin obscured the degree, through the liturgy, to which we share a common patrimony with the Orthodox, and to some extent, with England and some of the Lutheran countries.

A relevant preaching on poverty, particularly in the countries of greater affluence, is sorely needed. In keeping with such preaching, the style of life of the shepherd should be in conformity with the poor of his flock; it is hard to understand a pastor who drives around in a Cadillac while he has families in his parish that cannot pay their doctor bills. Surely, no priest wishes to live ostentatiously; the problem is to insure that the economic level of the priest should not exceed that of his average parishioner.

As far as question number 3 is concerned, it is important to keep in mind that although the Council is a legislative body which can make laws and put teeth into existing law that has not been applied, there is still the problem of bringing the majority of Catholics to observe them, and not simply their letter. Unfortunately, the Christian world is still in a preparatory stage on the road to unity, largely because of the persistence of prejudice and misinformation which is widespread in all denominations. Protestants are ignorant of the Catholic faith and still believe we are collecting weapons in the basements of our churches, and Catholics prefer to exert pressure against the TV showing of a movie on Luther rather than to learn the real causes of the Reformation or the schism of 1059. How many Catholics know about the sack of Constantinople in all its hideous reality?

We must act out what is in our hearts. The personal invitation by the Pope to Orthodox Patriarchs and the heads of Protestant churches —even as observers, and without voting rights—might well be a contribution to the cleansing of the century-old atmosphere of mutual suspicion. Needless to say, such actions have nothing to do with a public relations campaign to "sell" a "new image" of Catholicism; they must grow out of the humble recognition by Catholics, not only of our individual failures as sinful Christians, but of what the Church has suffered from its separation from the Christian East in the 11th century, and of much of Northern and Western Europe in the 16th. It is not only a question of numbers. Horizons were narrowed, emphases were misplaced, fountains of great strength and richness and beauty were closed. It is not that the theologically correct formulas regarding the Church as a perfect society, already existing in a divinely guaranteed unity, need to be abandoned. It is rather that our concern must be for the concrete realities of the tragedy of divided Christendom, in which the Church can be thought of as limping on one leg, and with only one arm to rule the souls of the faithful. We tend to think too exclusively of the fullness of the sacramental life which the Church has preserved, and which we wish to see available to our separated brothers; there is also the matter of what we have to gain, spiritually, from the different Christian traditions which they represent, gifts to be placed on the altar of unity which are irreplaceable, and which only they can provide.

Perhaps we do not need to repeat so often that no doctrinal concession is necessary. Our Christian brothers who today are looking at Rome with new interest have no more desire to treat the Revelation entrusted to the Church as a negotiable item than we have. But Catholic concern for the preservation of doctrine need not lead to an unwillingness to attempt to reformulate certain inevitably inadequate verbalizations regarding the mysteries of faith. A convenient example might well be the notion of hylomorphism. As applied to the Blessed Sacrament, we seem to end up with words which neither explain nor visualize what occurs. *Substance,* as used in theology, refers to a spiritual quality, and is not to be understood in terms of everyday language. Some theologians even attempt to distinguish between the molecular and atomic structure of the bread and wine that are used in Mass. This would appear to be bordering on blasphemy; it certainly is not increasing veneration for the Blessed Sacrament. A destructive attitude to the theories of St. Thomas and the great scholastics is neither useful nor called for; what we must do is transcend the attitude—which is alien to St. Thomas—that realities can be finally contained in formulas. The task is to approach the requirements of faith more closely by employing the original words of Christ. The Eucharist is a mystery which we can accept only in faith.

In this connection again, the contribution of the Orthodox tradition, which is as old as our own, can be considerable. Orthodox reluctance to emphasize dogmatic formulas has nothing to do with modern philosophical relativism. The Orthodox believe in the return of Our Lady to Christ after death but were disturbed at the doctrinal definition of the Assumption. We must watch to see that the explicit formulations of modern Catholic Mariology do not encourage Monophysite tendencies; in certain areas some Catholics seem no longer to regard Christ as the unique Mediator, but tend to act as if in practice He has delegated this to His Mother. Even though the official teaching of the Church would maintain the traditional dogmatic structure intact, this shift of emphasis is disturbing.

Precisely at the time when Christianity seems to have contracted to a relatively small area of the world in which the percentage of the non-Christian population is constantly increasing, and when Christianity seems on the defensive even in the old western nations that represent a bygone Christendom, the Church needs more than ever to recover its missionary *élan*. Every parish should regard itself not only in terms of its responsibility to the whole Church, but also as on permanent mission to the total community within its geographical limits. This has nothing to do with proselytizing or an exaggerated concern for statistical gains; it has everything to do with a conscious departure from the ghetto of excessive Catholic organizationalism toward an increased acceptance of responsibility and service in the life of the City. This desire may appear like vague romanticism to those concerned with the need for more religious vocations. Certainly we will have to adopt a policy which would expedite the redistribution of the clergy. Populous Catholic dioceses with few priests should be reinforced by minority Catholic dioceses which may have more priests than needed. Greater freedom and maneuverability could be gained by having the administration of a diocese, under a bishop and his archdeacon or chancellor, increasingly taken over by lay people. With deacons from the parishes, one or two priests might well be sufficient for each parish, increasing the possibility for an enormous missionary effort to countries in need of priests, without too great a sacrifice for the spiritual development of the home country.

It is hard for any of us to listen attentively to the directions of the Holy Spirit, and surely all Christians who understand the desire of Christ "that they all may be one" should find no difficulty in praying for the Fathers of the Council that they be given help in discharging their awesome responsibilities. And surely, too, though we should avoid wishful thinking and vague simplifications of all problems in terms of "a miracle of love," and recognize that the Council can by itself only constitute a first stage in Christian renewal, this is all the more reason for all of us, whether part of the magisterium or simple laymen, whether Catholic, Orthodox, or Protestant, to show a little more of that special sanity which is called holy impatience.

John Meyendorff

Orthodoxy and the Council

Pope John XXIII's announcement of the Council seemed to most Christians a revolutionary event in itself. Many, inside as well as outside the Roman Church, thought that the decisions of 1870 were irreconcilable with the idea of councils. Since there was already in existence a visible organ of infallibility which, in conformity with the conscience of the Church, could express *ex sese* the verities of the faith; since, moreover, this organ was invested with immediate jurisdiction over all faithful Catholics and could thus guide them directly and permanently in all the problems of Christian conscience in the modern world—what reason was there for holding a Council?

The manner in which the announcement was made, by the pope himself, on his own initiative and before Vatican officials could make a preliminary study of possible repercussions, accentuated still further the effect of surprise. In fact, it does not seem that John XXIII was posing the problem of whether the holding of a Council was reconcilable with Vatican dogma, but that he was simply affirming the fact that the conciliary institution was an integral part of Catholic ecclesiology and that Vatican dogma must be interpreted in terms of this permanent and necessary state of affairs. His various declarations relative to the Council, his desire to accentuate his own function as "bishop of Rome," a local bishop, "brother" of all the bishops of the world—Pius XII, on the contrary, used to emphasize his "universal episcopate"—and, finally, his desire to pose the problem of Christian unity in a new way, all showed that John XXIII was insisting upon a true return to the sources of Christian tradition.

In the Orthodox world reactions were numerous and on the whole sympathetic. That reservations and criticisms were also heard was only natural after centuries of mutual ignorance and often justified distrust and in the face of actual political circumstances. It remains true, none-

Father John Meyendorff is professor of Patristics and Church History at St. Vladimir's Orthodox Theological Seminary in New York. He is the author of INTRODUCTION A L'ÉTUDE DE GRÉGOIRE PALAMAS *(Seuil),* L'EGLISE ORTHODOXE HIER ET AUJOURD'HUI *(Seuil), and* ST. GRÉGOIRE PALAMAS ET LA MYSTIQUE ORTHODOXE *(Seuil).*

theless, that the Orthodox Church, since the time of the separation, has asked the West to question itself on the medieval developments of its theology and ecclesiology and judge them in accordance with the most ancient tradition. Certain Orthodox spokesmen of the last century sometimes even dreamed of a pope's proclaiming *ex cathedra* his own non-infallibility and thus assuring union of the churches. We have obviously not yet reached that point, but it is clear that the present pope is not content merely to wish for union; rather, he conceives of unity as a problem both external and internal to the Church of Rome. In convoking the Council he is trying to create, within the Roman Church itself, the conditions under which the union of Christians may become possible. It is in this self-questioning by the Catholic Church that there lies the great hope of unity.

The Roman West and Orthodoxy hold in common the idea that in the Incarnation Christ, by becoming historic man, wished for the existence on earth of a visible community—as visible as His own humanity—to which He promised a Spirit which would guide it in truth. This idea of a Church one and infallible was the common heritage of East and West throughout the first millennium of Christian history. What divides us today is above all the gigantic ecclesiological development produced in the West since the Gregorian reformation. Even in the seventh century, according to Pope Gregory the Great († 604), the idea of a "universal bishop"—the pope thus interpreted the title of "ecumenical patriarch" which had just been conferred upon the archbishop of Constantinople—was "a rash pretension which disturbed the peace of the entire Church,"[1] "a blasphemy attributing to a single bishop a dignity which suppressed that of all the rest."[2] Since then, in the West, the title of "universal bishop" has not only become common usage; it has really transformed the faith since the first Vatican Council: the jurisdiction of the pope over the assembly of the faithful of the universal Church is a jurisdiction that is "immediate" and "truly episcopal."

An evolution, or, as the theologians say, a "development of dogma" has indisputably occurred, therefore; on its part, the Christian East has not followed. A truth considered as only implicit in the first centuries of the Church was to become progressively explicit and finally definitive in 1870. Modern Catholic apologists like to collect citations from the Fathers and from Councils indicating the widespread understanding, in East and West alike, of Roman infallibility in ancient times. The Orthodox willingly admit that these florilegia indicate the reality of a certain authority for the Roman Church: they speak of a "preeminence of honor," of "prestige," and of "priority" in the common affairs of local churches; they recognize that these ideas would benefit from precise for-

---

1 Migne, *Patrologia latina,* 77, col. 739A.
2 *Ibid,* 746 C.

mulation by modern Orthodox theology, and that they constitute an important ecclesiological problem for the Church today.[3] But the Orthodox affirm an essential fact of the life of the ancient Church: when a question of faith was posed for Christians, its resolution was the province of the conscience *of all* the local churches. Concilary procedure was then resorted to. Once the question was settled—with the active or passive participation of Rome, sometimes without that participation—the discussions very often *continued:* they were terminated either by the disappearance of the heresy, by an authoritative commentary on the definition which satisfied the malcontents, or, finally, by schism. The *criterion* was always *truth itself,* and not a visible organ of infallibility.

This absence of a juridical criterion made a Christian of the first centuries a man both free and responsible. His freedom, moreover, was not a formal freedom of the individual: for a Christian there is no freedom outside truth, outside Christ and the Holy Spirit, outside the Church. But the Church, for the primitive Christian, was above all a *communion* and not an exterior criterion of doctrinal security. The primitive Christian was an active member of a living body; in the life of this body resided the miracle of infallibility and permanence. In the sacramental reality of the Eucharist, fully realized in every local community, communion to the Catholic body of the Church was accessible to all through baptism, in union with the saints of the past and in unity with all those who shared the same fidelity in Christ. The men who were invested with the *magisterium*—the bishops—were themselves in the service of this communion; they were its principal ministers but they did not in themselves determine it; they had to accomplish *within* the Church, not above it, their ministry as guardians of the apostolic tradition.

The preeminence of the Roman Church of the first centuries, recognized and in part defined by the ancient councils, was itself one of the *instruments* of this communion. When, in the Middle Ages, this preeminence became a definitive criterion, the whole ecclesiological perspective was modified. Soon an important part of Western Christianity felt itself deprived of fundamental Christian liberty and was driven into revolt. The Protestant revolt was followed by many others, still more negative ones, all of which opposed the Church in the name of freedom. The Church more and more identified itself with the idea of unconditional and infallible authority. This identification was the more patent as the Roman Church, in the face of the revolts, became more and more rigid: the Church defined, codified, and passed legislation upon the Mystery to try to protect it; at last the definition of infallibility

---

3 See on this subject a collection of recent articles by a group of Orthodox theologians, *La primauté de Pierre dans l'Église orthodoxe*, Paris. Neuchâtel, Delachaux, 1960; also *St. Vladimir's Quarterly*, vol. 4, 1960, No. 2-3, a volume dedicated to *Primacy and primacies.*

and immediate jurisdiction appeared. Purely human elements, of a social and political kind, played a well-known role in this last definition.

Reformation and Counter-Reformation thus set off a long chain reaction, which in large measure defined the history of Western Christianity in the last four centuries.

Has John XXIII mounted the throne of Peter to arrest this movement, which has been in process since Gregory VII, and to give it a less desperate direction? The forthcoming Council will be called upon to answer this question.

Modern Catholic "unionism" is connected, in the main, with three modes of thinking, which define three methods practiced in approaching the Orthodox.

1) A small group of theologians adheres quite simply to the old polemical method which consists in showing that the adversary is completely inconsistent and can only inspire a charitable pity. It is obvious that this attitude leaves all encounters at an impasse.

2) A second group of theologians and ecumenists affirms, on the contrary, that there are only misunderstandings between Orthodoxy and Rome; no serious doctrinal difference keeps the two great historic churches of the East and the West in opposition. When others attempt to raise questions of dogma, this group even questions their intentions: why create problems, as long as the Orthodox can find in embryo in their own Eastern tradition all the doctrine which Rome has explicitly formulated? All that is needed to create unity is for the two parties to change their psychological attitude and abandon their prejudices and misunderstandings. At this point Roman centrality will appear a providential instrument which gives the Church the necessary flexibility to integrate—within itself, naturally—those different rituals and traditions, whose very variety and multiplicity constitute the best sign of true catholicity.

3) A third group, while generally sharing the desire for greater openness characteristic of the preceding group, differs from it on one essential point. They admit the enormous doctrinal and institutional problem represented, for the Orthodox, by the Roman Church in its present state; they share this difficulty from inside and wish the Roman positions to be reformulated, if not modified; this desire stems not from a special "interest in problems of unity"; rather, it is a desire to see the Church of Christ as Christ wanted it to be. This attitude springs from a truly theocentric spirituality common to all, Catholic or non-Catholic, who are concerned with bearing Christian witness in the modern world and do not believe that everything can be solved by ecclesiastical politics. With theologians of this spirit, the Orthodox will not be ashamed to make a self-criticism and recognize the historic deficiencies of his own Church; he will be ready to share in the search for the single truth.

Under the pontificate of Pius XII the Roman attitude was largely determined by the first group and to a certain degree by the second. The really new aspect of the conduct of John XXIII is that the pope himself seems to belong to the third. His personal friendships before the pontificate (notably that which allied him to Dom Beauduin Lambert), his experience of Eastern Christian affairs, and the numerous public disavowals he has addressed to polemicists and denigrators, constitute the great hope of the Council over which he is soon to preside.

It is obvious that everything will not be resolved at this assembly. There will be no discussion of *Filioque,* of original sin, or of sacramental theology. There will be discussion, it seems, above all of the Church. In this respect the success or failure of the council—on the unionist level —will depend upon the content of the additions which can (or cannot) be borne by the definitions of 1870. Two examples may be cited here, as they have already been mentioned in the Catholic press itself: 1) Infallibility *ex cathedra* and *ex sese, non autem ex consensu ecclesiae;* 2) "Immediate" and "truly episcopal" jurisdiction by the pope over all the faithful.

The dogma of infallibility aroused furious polemic before and after its publication; Pius IX himself after the Council partly moderated its effect in his correspondence with the German bishops. It is rather generally admitted that the redaction of the dogma is unfortunate, in the degree to which absolute and, for many, frightening terminology like "infallibility" and *ex sese,* is used in a rather imprecise context. These terms can be understood in the most "integralist" sense, though they are susceptible of moderate interpretation. Thus the possible distinction between *consensus* and *sensus ecclesiae* is invoked: in excluding the *consensus ecclesiae* from the conditions requisite to a definition of infallibility, the Vatican Council simply wished to discard the juridical idea of a majority and "democratic" vote. As to the *sensus ecclesiae,* this vital and organic aspect of the Church, which has always been identical with itself since apostolic times, here the pope would be submissive, like the other bishops and like all Christians, both in his *ex cathedra* statements as in his other acts.[4] An interpretation of the definition of 1870 along this line would certainly open a very large door to subsequent dialogue between Rome and Orthodoxy. Because, finally, for the Orthodox Church, too, the seat of infallibility is not the majority vote; it is, rather, this *sensus ecclesiae* which is fundamentally nothing other than the Holy Spirit dwelling in the Church.

The problem of immediate jurisdiction—a less noted and less discussed aspect of the decisions of 1870—apparently presents difficulties at least as great as those of infallibility.[5] The text assumes in effect that the

---

[4] *Cf.* on this subject, R. Aubert, "L'ecclésiologie du concile du Vatican," in *Le Concile et les conciles* (Cerf), 1960, p. 281.

[5] *Ibid,* pp. 283–4.

pope exercises his function as universal pastor directly over all the faithful and for this does not need the bishops even as intermediaries. A certain tendency in modern Catholic ecclesiology even suggests the possibility of a still greater limitation of the role of the episcopate, a functional institution whose immediate utility might eventually disappear. The Holy See with the aid of the religious orders would be able to provide for the whole administration of the universal Church. This is obviously not a question of the official interpretation of the dogma of 1870 but of a possible development of the decision on "immediate jurisdiction." On the practical level, in any case, "immediate jurisdiction" renders the Catholic Church suspect in all countries where the political philosophy does not correspond to that advanced by the Roman encyclicals.

This seems to have been what limited John F. Kennedy's majority to 100,000 votes in the American Presidential elections of November, 1960. It also permitted Rome to suppress the experiment of the worker-priests in France, without the French bishops being able seriously to undertake the defense of this particular aspect of their pastoral concern for the flock which God confided to them. The problem of the episcopate, which the first Vatican Council did not have time to examine, will be of primary importance for this one. A viable definition will be sought, on the one hand, for the traditional bond between the bishop and his diocese and, on the other, for the relation between the bishops and Rome. The definition the Catholic Church gives to its own internal structure will in large measure determine the perspectives of Christian unity. The Orthodox Church for its part has always confessed the impossibility of a bishop's exercising a power of divine right over another bishop or over the community presided over by another bishop; Orthodox ecclesiology is in fact founded upon the essential identity—in a single sacramental reality and a single apostolic succession—of all the local churches.

Clearly it will not be easy for the fathers of the Second Vatican Council to bring important correctives to bear upon the decisions of 1870. The centralized structure which under Pius IX received absolute dogmatic and religious foundation confers—apparently, at least—a formidable efficacy upon the Roman Catholic Church. Can one light-heartedly renounce even a part of that efficacy? And the Orthodox Church, in its contemporary aspect, is far from being able to serve in all things as a very attractive model. However, when it is a matter of the religion of the Gospels, the problem of efficacy can no longer be treated as it is on the human level. The efficacy of the Spirit of God does not obey the laws of worldly success: the existence, in 1961, of millions of Orthodox Christians in Russia proves that the life of the Church does not depend upon political systems or upon ecclesiastical centralizations built up in the Middle Ages. And, finally, is not the problem of our time one of detachment with regard to the philosophical, social, or political doctrines which are collapsing under our eyes? In recognizing this collapse we obviously risk accepting as absolute the new systems which are now taking form; one easily becomes modernist by merging with bad alloys. But it is certainly not an indication of modernism to return to the sources of the Christian tradition, in order to find there the absolute and permanent kernel of truth. Such a return is the condition of unity.

translated by ELIZABETH STAMBLER

Stephen Neill

An Anglican Plea for Clear Answers

The news that the pope had decided to call a Council was such as to surprise and even shock a large number of Christians all over the world. Maybe this was the main reason why the news was so well received; it seemed highly unlikely that we would see such an event come to pass in our time, and all at once we were told it would soon take place.

As far as I am concerned, I had the opportunity some years ago to make a detailed study of the Council of Trent and the Vatican Council, which led me to the conclusion that a new Council would never be convoked. It was clear that these Councils had been, in the strict sense, Councils of the Pope. It was he who had directed them in all their details, and succeeded in obtaining from them the decisions he had at heart. Since the pope has now been proclaimed infallible and endowed with the power of publishing the will of God on all subjects relating to faith and morals, would it not be simpler for him to save the expense and trouble of a Council and simply give the directives that he judges necessary—after consulting, of course, the bishops and theologians? In fact, of the three dogmas recently proclaimed, two, the Immaculate Conception and the bodily Assumption of the Blessed Virgin Mary, have been promulgated without the formalities of a Council. It may very well also be that the pope himself, when he launched the idea, did not have a clear conception of the immense labor and considerable expense that a Council would involve. Those of us who have collaborated in the preparation of international Christian conferences know very well all that this implies. To have all the bishops come to Rome, to put them up there comfortably, to find something for each of them to do, to lead them to agreement and to translate this agreement in good and due form—all this constitutes a task next to which the labor of Sisyphus is only child's play.

But now the decision has been taken and the Council will take place.

The Very Rev. Stephen Neill, D.D., former bishop of Tinnevelly, South India, is the author (with Ruth Rouse) of the History of the Ecumenical Movement *(Westminster). He is professor of missions and ecumenical theology at the Colgate-Rochester Divinity School and the editor of* World Christian Books.

It cannot fail to be an event of the greatest interest for the history of the Church in the 20th century. Nevertheless, no matter how interesting an event is, it does not, simply because of that, have great significance. It would be quite possible for the Council to take place without showing itself very meaningful. It is almost certain that it will leave an imprint on the interior life of the Roman Church, but this will perhaps be accomplished without leaving the slightest trace in the life of other churches, and without bringing any contribution to the closer unity among the children of Christ which we all invoke in our wishes, and let us hope, in our prayers.

Will the Council take on great significance? This will depend on whether or not it will deal directly with a certain number of grave problems and make perfectly clear and unequivocal declarations in regard to them. The other churches want to know exactly where they stand as regards the Roman Catholic Church. Pious and soothing talks in favor of unity and Christian charity contribute nothing new; we have all heard enough of them. And equivocal statements would be worse than none at all.

I

First of all, it would be necessary for the Council to spell out clearly its own status. Just exactly what is a Council of the Roman Church today? What authority does it possess, if it has one?

We know exactly where we are when it is a matter of the World Council of Churches, or of the Lambeth Conference which brings Anglican bishops together. Neither of these organisms pretends to be a synod nor to fix directives for the Churches. They are only consultative assemblies. Their resolutions have no other value than that conferred on them by the light of the spiritual wisdom to which they bear witness. We also know where we stand in regard to the synod of a Church that is provided with a democratic constitution. In India, I was a member of the General Council of the Church of India, Burma, and Ceylon (the Anglican Church in the Indies) and president of my diocesan synod. Each of these organizations got together to fill official tasks, and their decisions committed those Churches comprised by their respective jurisdictions.

To which of these categories does a Council of the Roman Church belong? It may be useful to ask the question in this emphatic form, not with any intention to offend, but simply because a question that has been sharply posed has more chance of receiving a clear answer. For those who have read the canons of the Vatican Council concerning infallibility, it would appear that the assembled bishops could unanimously declare themselvs in favor of a certain declaration regarding faith and morals, but that the Pope, in the name of his authority alone, could say "No" to what the episcopacy profoundly desired. Inversely, the entire company of bishops might consider a particular proposition inopportune, undesirable, or even positively heretical, but the Pope could, nevertheless, declare that it was part of the doctrine that the Church must believe for its eternal salvation, and all the bishops would be immediately compelled to abandon all their objections and accept the Pope's decision. Of course, it can be said that such a thing will probably never happen. But there is a whole world of difference between the words "improbable" and "impossible," and it is precisely on this point that the world and the Church require a clear answer. Is the Council only a deliberative assembly? Or does it possess of itself a certain spiritual authority? If the latter, how is this authority to be reconciled with that of the Pope who convoked the Council, who will doubtless preside over certain of its meetings, and without whose *placet* none of the suggestions formulated by the Council could be effective?

II

Next we would be glad to hear a straightforward declaration concerning the status of those who participate in the Council. It is believed that the majority will be bishops. But what does it mean to be a bishop today in the Roman Church? As is known, the Anglican Churches firmly believe that they have preserved the catholic episcopacy in all its purity, but tend to believe that the Vatican Council abolished it in the Roman Church.

The idea that every Anglican bishop has a function does not present the slightest obscurity: he is the representative of Christ in a particular district in which he is entrusted with watching especially over the Anglican flock that lives there, but also to bear witness, to the degree that it is possible for him, before all the other inhabitants of that area, whether they be non-Christians or members of other Christian communions. Of course, he has been raised to his function by the vote of his flock (very democratically, in the Indies) and his election has been confirmed by other bishops of his province. He has been consecrated by at least three bishops (on this matter our Church is more strict than the Roman; since the Reformation no consecration has in fact taken place without the presence of at least three bishops). Our bishop is required to act in close connection with the rest of the episcopacy and he swears an oath of obedience to his Metropolitan. Nevertheless, he does not have the slightest doubt that it is Christ who has chosen him for this high function, and that he is responsible directly to Christ.

Let us see now what idea a Roman Catholic bishop makes of his situation. The bishop of Rome has been proclaimed the universal pastor of the faithful and their judge in all causes, from the largest to the smallest. What then is the status of the bishop? Is he the local representative of the bishop of Rome? Or is he still, in a certain sense, the local representative of Christ? If the latter, in what sense? And what relation is there between his pastoral responsibility and that exercised by the bishop of Rome over all the faithful, whether taken collectively or individually? Doubtless each of these questions admits of a response, but there would be considerable value in having these responses clearly expressed. To the degree in which reconciliation with the Anglican churches may be considered, it is essential not to leave even the slightest doubt as to the fully catholic character of the episcopacy of the Roman Church.

The Council will surely discuss a large number of questions which concern only the interior affairs of the Roman Church. We do not yet know under what forms and in what context the problem of union among the dispersed children of Christ will come into discussion. What is almost sure, however, is that in one manner or another it will be discussed. Because of this, certain problems of interest will be posed for other Christian communions.

III

What is the official point of view of the Roman Church concerning the status of believers in good faith of the other Christian Churches? We have noticed in recent years the adoption of a much more irenic and generous attitude to us on the part of distinguished Catholic personalities. They prefer to speak of us now as "separated brothers," and as someone has remarked, today they tend to put the accent on "brothers" rather than on "separated." All this is fine and good. Nevertheless, considerable differences can be noted among the opinions expressed by Roman Catholics themselves as to the meaning which should be attached to the word "brothers." It is on this point, perhaps, more than any other, that a clear and unambiguous declaration would be necessary. We desire to know what we really are.

The point of departure, I suppose, is the sacrament of Baptism. The Roman Church recognizes the validity of baptism administered in the other Churches on condition that it has been performed with water and in the name of the Holy Trinity. This means that, for example, all Anglicans are validly baptized from even the strictest Roman Catholic point of view, and are hence an integral part of the Church which is the Body of Christ. Many of them also believe firmly in all the doctrines of Catholic faith set forth in the Nicene Creed. Many of them lead an exemplary life. When they sin, they do not receive absolution from a priest of the Roman Church, but they try to practice the perfect contrition which makes pardon possible by virtue of the merits and mediation of the Son of God. How does the Roman Church look on such Christians? If in a certain sense they are part of the Church, then they must be considered as on the road to eternal salvation. If they cannot be considered as part of the Church, it becomes difficult to see what their baptism means. Here again there is no doubt that these questions find clear answers within Roman theology, but if they were decided once and for all without any possible ambiguity or quibbling, many doubts and agonies would be appeased.

The occasion should also be taken for authority to apply itself to a minor, but nevertheless important, subject. As I said, Anglicans are validly baptized. That is why, when some of them wish to become Roman Catholics, there should be no question of re-baptizing them. The repetition of a sacrament implies blasphemy or desecration. A well-known case is that of Robert Hugh Benson, son of a former Archbishop of Canterbury; he absolutely refused to permit his baptism to be questioned and was accepted on these terms in the Roman Church. But desecration has taken place too frequently in circumstances which lead us to ask if some Roman Catholic priests have ever been instructed in the exact nature of a sacrament. If the Council solemnly declared that in the future such a desecration would be forbidden and that disciplinary sanctions would be applied against those who broke the rules, much good would result. (We should note that Roman Catholics who become Anglicans are not re-baptized if they can bring documentary proof that they have already received the sacrament.)

IV

One of the principal questions to be raised at the Council will be religious freedom. Here again simple formulas and pious explanations will not be enough to produce any effect. It is rapid action that is desired and awaited. I will take only one example: the situation of the minority Churches in Spain is absolutely intolerable. Most of the privileges of citizenship are denied to the members of Protestant communities. Since Roman Catholics claim religious freedom for their minorities in countries like Finland, they should be prepared to accept the converse. It is sometimes objected on this point that, being in possession of the total Truth, the Roman Church could not permit the existence nor the propagation of error in cases in which it is possible to prevent it. It is extremely important that a Roman Catholic should not lose sight of the fact that, in the eyes of Anglicans, it is the Roman Church which teaches grave error, and that they are nevertheless ready to fight to the end to assure their Catholic fellow-citizens a complete freedom in the exercise of their faith. It is very largely due to the efforts of Anglicans that the Emancipation Act for Roman Catholics was voted in 1829, and the noteworthy fact that the Catholic John F. Kennedy was chosen president of the United States in a country with a Protestant majority, goes to demonstrate the seriousness of the position of the Protestants when they claim themselves partisans of religious freedom for others as well as themselves.

Roman Catholics sometimes forget the gravity of this problem in non-Christian countries which have recently gained their independence. From the Islamic point of view, the Roman Church, along with the other Christian Churches, spreads grave errors which should be condemned. To some degree, we have so far succeeded in assuring for ourselves a certain missionary freedom of action by emphasizing that the vast majority of western nations grant non-Christians complete freedom to practice and propagate their faith. When a Moslem state tried to prevent its Christian residents from enjoying freedom of worship, the State Department at Washington threatened to close that city's mosque as reprisal. Freedom was at once assured for American citizens residing abroad.

The Roman Catholic position, especially in Spain but also in other countries, harms the cause of Christians the world over. In fact, if we do not practice religious freedom among Christians, we have no solid basis for trying to claim it for ourselves or our brothers of related confessions who live in non-Christian countries. Of course, it is impossible to set up overnight a program of action which the Franco government would be obliged to execute, but surely if the Council took a clear and firm position on the policy to be followed, it would have an immense influence on the situation. The least action directed at abolishing the restrictions which disturb Spanish Protestants in the practice of their faith would arouse a more profound world-wide current of confidence in the sincerity of Roman statements on behalf of Unity than any number of declarations not followed by an act in this direction.

V

Let us mention quickly a problem which has particular interest for Anglicans. It is known that in 1896 the Bull *Apostolicae Curae* of Leo XIII condemned Anglican ordinations and consecrations as invalid and declared them null and void.

There has already been too long a delay in reopening this question. The general opinion of Anglicans on this bull is that it *may have* succeeded in showing that episcopal succession and ordinations in their Church are invalid, but that *most of all* it demonstrated that the Roman Church has neither succession nor valid ordinations. Many Roman Catholics feel embarrassed by this bull, but naturally, in the name of obedience, they feel obliged to accept it as long as it has not been corrected. But historical and theological scholarship has studied this question and it may be said with assurance that no pope today would issue a bull composed in such terms. I can do no better than to cite two sentences of Bishop A. S. Headlam, written forty years ago: "One has rarely seen a pope or any other controversialist present propositions whose falsity has been proved in such a decisive matter by later studies as these of Leo XIII. . . . It would be good, perhaps, to explain that if we, who are members of the Church of England, insist that the Roman Church recognize our ordinations, it is not because we have the slightest doubt of their validity, but because we would be happy to see the Roman Church take a decision in conformity with the principles of Truth and Charity."[1]

A way of reopening the question could easily be found. It has never been claimed that Leo XIII's bull possessed an infallible character. It represents the judgment by the Pope at a certain moment of history, in the light of the documents which were available to him at that time. The history of the Roman Church offers numerous examples of previous decisions which were reconsidered, the most famous being the one by Pius VII restoring the Jesuit order in 1814, even though the bull of dissolution published by Clement XIV in 1773 had specified that this question was never to be raised by any of his successors. Naturally, it is impossible to predict what would result from a reconsideration of Anglican ordination by the Roman authorities. What is important is that it be studied in a climate of frankness and honesty, with concern only to establish the truth. In practice it is clear that no other initiative would bring as efficacious a contribution to progress toward Christian unity as a declaration of Rome in favor of the validity and canonical regularity of Anglican ordinations. Of course, the Council may not treat this question itself, but it could start the process which might then continue for several years before being completed.

Among the minor subjects on which there is interest in seeing the Council take a decision, there is one which is of special interest among Anglicans. It is a well-known fact that since the Accord of Bonn, signed in 1931, interconsecration is regularly practiced among the Old Catholic and Anglican Churches. This means that a little more than half of the Anglican bishops have issued both from the Old Catholic and the Anglican succession, and it is probable that more than half the Anglican ministers today have been ordained by bishops descending from this succession. The Roman Church considers Old Catholic consecrations valid, although irregular. From the Roman Catholic point of view, then, what is the status of the Anglican bishops and priests who have received the ministry through this avenue common to Old Catholics and Anglicans? Many Roman Catholics hold that, because of this situation, the Anglican communion now possesses a certain percentage of valid ordinations and ministers (although schismatic, naturally), and that soon all its bishops and clergy will have received orders, which, in principle, are recognized by Rome as valid. As far as I know, no official declaration

---

1 *The Doctrine of the Church and Reunion*, p. 253 and p. 248, note 1.

on this subject has ever been published. Even if a favorable judgment were pronounced, this would not in itself immediately produce a degree of intercommunion between our two Churches. It would be first necessary to work to eliminate serious doctrinal differences which separate us. Nevertheless, the perspective for union would have been brought considerably closer. It seems that a Council would be completely qualified to make a synodal declaration on a subject of this kind.

VI

Another subject urgently in need of discussion is the relations among Christians of different confessions in the missionary territories of Asia, Africa, and elsewhere. Let us be frank and recognize that almost always relations are as bad as possible. Despite some happy exceptions, we can say that the situation is general. Serious faults have been committed on both sides. Where Roman Catholics arrived first, Protestants sometimes followed and began their campaign of evangelization by slurring their Catholic neighbors and by taking up discussions exactly on the points where there was the best chance of wounding the mind and conscience of the converts. The inverse case can also be found; where there were flourishing Protestant missions, Catholics often came to establish themselves. The result is a disastrous disunion, even in the tiniest islands lost in the immensity of the Pacific.

There is nothing imaginary about this. As a missionary bishop, I have experience of the harm done to the cause of Christ by the incapacity of his children to live side by side in respect and mutual loyalty. I will cite only one extreme example: in a village where the Christian community was part Anglican and part Catholic, the Anglicans woke up one fine morning and discovered that the Catholics had taken possession of their church. We have always tried to practice the commandment of Paul (I *Cor.* 6) not to bring suit against other Christians before the courts of non-believers; nevertheless, after all other means of conciliation failed, we could do nothing but open a case before civil courts in order to have the places restored to the community which had built them for the celebration of Anglican worship. The case was won, but cost great sums which might better have been spent elsewhere for the glory of God. After that, it was hardly possible to hope to see friendly relations reign in this village among the Christians of both camps, or to count on Hindus having much respect for a religion which cannot even keep peace between its adherents of different confessions. On the other hand, I am glad to point out that my relations with my neighbor bishop of Tuticorin, first Hindu bishop of the Latin rite in the modern period, have always been correct and friendly. We worked together so that, in the territory in which our jurisdictions overlap, scandals such as the one I just mentioned, would not take place. I regretted a great deal not being able to go to see him and get to know him personally. My predecessor did, but his visit was never returned, and my flock would naturally not want me to put myself in the position of seeing the same thing happen again. I did go to visit another neighbor, the bishop of Mandoura, and we had a very friendly conversation, but my successor was not able to do the same, for the reason which I mentioned above.

Many of us are pained by this lack of fraternal spirit, but it is not easy to see what to do in order to remedy it. By what means could we begin? It is difficult even for a Council to pass rules and regulations regarding matters which are, after all, related to personal attitudes and are in the area of simple courtesy. But the Council is going to bring together a large percentage of the bishops of the whole world. If these bishops could solemnly renounce, and commit their people to renounce, every unfriendly word or action toward other Christians (except to the degree in which controversy, conducted in a spirit of respect and affection, is a permanent fact in the life of the Church over the ages), and if, when they returned to their dioceses, they placed their good resolutions into practice, the effect would be enormous. Obviously, these good habits should be reciprocal. Protestants also have reproaches to address to themselves, and would do well, on many occasions, to adopt a more charitable and courteous attitude to their Roman brothers.

The question of proselytism has been studied for several years by a commission of the World Council of Churches, and understanding has been reached on a certain number of principles among representatives of different Churches. It would be splendid if the Council could declare itself in accord with these principles and recommend their observance in the whole Catholic world.

VII

It is not the business of a non-Catholic to suggest subjects regarding the interior life of the Church which the Council ought to study. Recent years have evidenced a revival of life within the Roman Church which other Christians have not failed to notice with the greatest satisfaction. The accent placed on the bible, its study by laymen, the publication of a veritable stream of numerous and excellent translations of the Catholic bible in many languages, the revival of a biblical preaching—all these are manifestations that an Anglican observer can only welcome with pious gratitude. In addition, there are many things in the liturgical revival which gladden his heart, and he feels that he himself has a great deal to learn from it. Naturally, he hopes that a day will come when the Roman Church will decide to accept the principle adopted with such eagerness by other Churches during the Reformation: the celebration of worship, including Mass, in the vernacular. But here again is a subject in which an outsider has no right to speak; it is an interior affair which should be decided by each church.

Nevertheless, there exist a certain number of theological subjects on which a sympathetic observer might dare to risk the hope that the Council would want to direct its attention.

Roman Catholics know very well that the central role given in recent years to the devotion to the Blessed Virgin Mary is one of the facts which most pain all those who love and admire the Roman Catholic Church without themselves being members of it. Theologically, the matter is easily explained. The Roman Church, like others, is convinced that everything that Mary has comes from her Divine Son. That is why, when theologians encourage the honoring of Mary, it is uniquely in order by this means to give greater honor to her Son. But it is difficult to believe that this is completely evident in the eyes of the ordinary faithful. It is obvious that the dogma of the Assumption of the Blessed Virgin could not be reconsidered; it was irrevocable. The great majority of Roman Catholics do not appear to be aware that the proclamation of this dogma has dug a new and deep ditch between them and the Christians of other confessions. If we ever get to the point of serious discussion of a union of Churches, this new and formidable barrier will appear terribly difficult for us to clear. For the moment, something else is more relevant. If the Council could make a solemn declaration on the absolute and incomparable supremacy of Christ, and the total subordination of Mary to Him, and do it in such clear terms that no misunderstanding was possible, it would be of the greatest utility in clarifying and purifying devotion to the Virgin in the Roman Church itself, and would greatly help in calming the concern of many outside that Church in regard to its theological tendencies.

Another theological question to which the Council would do well to give attention is that of the Holy Spirit. What strikes the reader of Roman Catholic theology is the almost total absence of a coherent doctrine concerning the action of the Holy Spirit in the Church and in the souls of believers. On this point all Churches are rather unsatisfactory, but the doctrine of Rome is more so than almost all others. Certainly, it preserves the orthodox formulation elaborated in the first centuries of Christianity, but when we think of the extremely important work done in recent years on the doctrine of the Mystical Body and the Eucharist, it may not be useless to suggest that it is time to make the Holy Spirit an essential theme of thought and theological study during the years after the conclusion of the Council.

A Council cannot treat large theological subjects with great depth; there is not enough time and the majority of bishops do not have the qualifications to create a really scientific theology. In the majority of cases, the latter only makes progress thanks to the long and patient work of isolated individuals, who succeed in gaining the veneration of the Church only because of their excellence. Nevertheless, a Council can have great influence in this area: instructions pointing out the various directions in which theological research might make progress will certainly receive the most careful and revered attention from scholars all over the world, and could serve as a point of departure for a new phase of theological development.

VIII

This Council will be essentially a council of the Roman Catholic Church. We do not know if non-Roman Catholics will be invited to attend it. Nor have the slightest indications been given on the conditions under which they might be able to be present. But the Fathers of the Council ought to know that the eyes of the whole world are fixed on them, and their deliberations will be followed with the greatest attention in all corners of the earth by Christians who are not part of the Roman confession. It will be highly regrettable if they take adequate cognizance of this fact and do not consider seriously enough the possibility of making real progress toward a greater comprehension and a closer union between all those who have been baptized in the name of the Father, Son, and Holy Spirit. The present pope and his predecessors have said noble words on this subject, but there is a great deal more to do.

The fact is that we do not know each other well at all, and the most serious misunderstandings continue to divide the Christian world. It is obvious that many Protestants know very little of the Roman Church, its doctrine and action. But I should say that, on the whole, Protestants are better informed on Roman Catholicism than Roman Catholics are on non-Roman Churches and their doctrines. Of course, I know many exceptions. I have Catholic friends who are very well informed on Anglicanism, and a Catholic priest even told me that when he was in England he always attended the Anglican service in the evening "because the sermons in your church are better than in ours." But such friends are rare. Only recently an English Catholic lady told me, "After all, your holy Communion is only a memorial, nothing more." I asked her, "Who taught you that?," and she answered that this is what she was taught at the convent school she attended. Undoubtedly the good nuns in question were only passing on to their students what they had been taught or what they had read somewhere. It is to be hoped that the period of ignorance and false information has now come to an end.

Here again the Council of itself cannot do a great deal, but it can exercise great influence. A heartfelt declaration recommending a more charitable attitude toward other Christians and a deliberate effort to understand better what each really believes would find a welcome response in all corners of the world. Many Roman Catholics are now beginning at last to have a fuller comprehension of Protestantism. Although their education tends to make them look at it in a purely negative way, they have now reached the point of conceding that one cannot even arrive at an elementary understanding of Protestantism unless one begins by accepting as a fundamental principle that the purpose and intention of every Protestant is to obey Christ in all things. If, in the name of this obedience, he felt firmly drawn to the Roman Church, he would follow this path without hesitation. And indeed, no Roman Catholic should want to see a Protestant become Catholic at the expense of what he considers demanded by his obedience to Jesus Christ.

The Council could exercise a profound and decisive influence on this point. At present, the formation which the vast majority of Roman Catholic priests receive in regard to non-Roman Churches is seriously deficient. Many have never read a single word on the theology of these churches. What they know has been picked up in out-dated manuals which are really inadequate today. In order to make progress on the path of ecumenism, we need to begin by learning to know, in a spirit of love and sympathy, what others profess, and what their Christian life can be. It is here that the Council's action can be decisive; firm, clear directives on this subject would be applied by superiors of all the seminaries who are in charge of the training of the clergy all over the world. Since many of the bishops who are members of the Council also have seminaries under their direction, it will be easy for them to see to it that the necessary improvements be made in the instruction of candidates for the priesthood.

Such are the tasks, it appears to me, which the Council should be asked to assume in the period in which we are now living, taking into consideration the needs of the Roman Church as much as those of the other Churches. But when all is said and done, what is going to be the result of all this? I have been involved in all kinds of ecclesiastical meetings for more than thirty years. I do not have great hope that a great deal of good comes out of them, although my pessimism is not as complete as that of St. Gregory Nazianzen when he said that he had never seen a council produce anything but harm!

There are three kinds of ecclesiastical assemblies:

——some are completely unimportant and leave no mark either in the life of the Church or in that of the world;

——others really do harm, either because they make ill-considered statements, or re-enforce existing prejudices;

——a few, very few, are truly profitable, because they deal with an important subject in a prophetic style and move the conscience of the Christian world in the direction of a greater loyalty and deeper devotion to Christ, or because they take effective decisions for the greater good of the Church and of humanity.

To which of these three categories will the next Council of Rome belong?

It appears probable to me that it will be the unimportant kind. My experience in the World Council of Churches and the Lambeth Conference suggests that a council of such amplitude requires two or three years to be put together. I would judge that the preparations made up till now are completely insufficient. I am very much afraid that the Council will produce only superficial declarations on subjects that people have not had the time to think through, and pious platitudes which, though appeasing the conscience of those who utter them, do not bring any help to the condition and problems of men and women living in the world today.

I even fear that it will do harm by strengthening still more that rigidity which has been getting worse within the Roman Church for the last four centuries.

I hope, nevertheless, that the Council will do some good by speaking in a courageous and effective way, by attacking some of the urgent problems of the life of the Church and the world, by encouraging a new current of theological thought, and contributing to a genuine reconciliation of spirit among all those whom the name of Christians unites, although they still live separated from one another.

But the dangers are very great. Hence it is of the highest importance that the avenues to the Council be prepared by an intense prayer, in particular by all those who will not be directly represented, but cannot fail to be interested in its work, since it is to be assembled in the name of Christ and call on the assistance of the Holy Spirit in its inaugural prayer.

Robert McAfee Brown

An American Protestant View

It is a strange feeling for a Protestant to be asked to comment on items that should be considered by a Roman Catholic Council. And while it is important not to be too sanguine about how many of one's suggestions will actually be adopted by those planning the Council, it is important also to recognize that even the invitation itself is significant. For the invitation signifies a new situation in Catholic-Protestant relationships that is very hopeful for the future. Not too long ago one would not have assumed that the Catholic Church would display any particular interest in what non-Catholics had to say on such a matter. But it is now clear both that non-Catholics have genuine interest and concern in the Council, and that the Catholic Church will listen to those concerns and treat them seriously.

My task as a Protestant is surely not to suggest ways in which the Council should give Catholicism a more Protestant tinge—a fruitless venture even if I felt it a worthy one—but to suggest some things that the Roman Catholic Church could do or say, in fidelity to its own understanding of the Christian faith, that would be signs of encouragement and hope to Protestants. There are a number of areas in which Protestants observe new stirrings on the Roman Catholic scene, and perhaps the most helpful thing the Ecumenical Council could do for us would be to clarify the place that these new stirrings have within the official life and voice of Roman Catholicism. One of the greatest difficulties I face as an American Protestant trying to urge fellow Protestants to a sympathetic understanding of Roman Catholicism, is that whenever I point to some movement of creativity within Catholic life or thought I am met by the comment, "Oh, but that's not typical," or "But that doesn't *really* represent the church, it's just a fringe movement with no official support whatever." Nevertheless, I have the feeling that a lot of things are going on in contemporary Catholic life that cannot properly be dismissed by such comments, because they are really taking root in the life of the Church. In what follows, therefore, I shall indicate some of the areas in which it would be most helpful to non-Catholics to have more

Robert Mc Afee Brown is the author of THE SPIRIT OF PROTESTANTISM *(Oxford) and (with Gustave Weigel)* AN AMERICAN DIALOGUE *(Anchor). He is professor of Theology at Union Theological Seminary in New York, where he gave a special seminar this year on contemporary Catholicism.*

definitive statements than we now possess about certain aspects of Roman Catholic life and thought. Statements on these matters coming from an ecumenical council would be far more helpful to us than statements merely by individual Catholics, on which we now have to rely in large measure.

I

The issue over which there is the greatest fuzziness of understanding, and also the greatest unrest, on the part of American non-Catholics, centers on the Church's attitude to toleration and religious liberty. What is the "real" stand of the church on this matter? Proponents of either a "hard" or a "soft" line can produce documentation to support their own interpretation of the Church's position. And yet the most impressive documentation comes from those who believe that the Church still holds rather rigidly to the "thesis-hypothesis" view of the matter, i.e., that toleration is not a right the Catholic Church should extend to others when it is in the majority, but that it is a right the Catholic Church should demand for itself when it is in the minority. Statements of a different view (a view, for example, that religious toleration is not based on expediency but on a true understanding of faith) are expressed only here and there by individuals. They do not seem to have clear sanction or official support. Thus Roman Catholic statements favoring toleration tend to be dismissed by American non-Catholics as either meaningless or inconsequential in the light of the more "official" statements of a contrary position, and the awesome evidence of the repressive actions of the church against minorities in places where it has preponderant power.

There is, to be sure, a brief paragraph in *Mystici Corporis* (para. 104), and there is Pius XII's *Speech to the Italian Jurists* of December 6, 1953, and there are perhaps a few more emanating from high places that seem to encourage a new position—but these are so very few when compared to the abundance of contrary evidence that can be produced! Protestants have been immensely helped by the compilation of Carillo de Albornoz, *Roman Catholicism and Religious Liberty*, issued under the sponsorship of the World Council of Churches, which documents the widespread dissatisfaction in many Catholic circles with the "thesis-hypothesis" theory, and cites constructive Catholic alternatives to it. But once again, more than a compilation of individual opinions is needed. What is needed is clearer light by official voices within the church as to the present status of the question of toleration and religious liberty.

Observers of the American scene will recall the acrimony and discord over the so-called "Catholic issue" that marked the 1960 presidential campaign. No matter how often Mr. Kennedy asserted his belief in principles of liberty and toleration, no matter how often he deplored the notion of preferential treatment for his own Church, he was greeted by the assertion that although his statements were admirable they were untypical, that in these respects he was not a "good Catholic," and that once he was in power the Church would persuade him to adopt an attitude more in keeping with the Spanish pattern. Thus far Mr. Kennedy has exhibited an admirable unwillingness to change his position, and he has thus assuaged the initial fears of a large segment of American Protestantism. But there is still a feeling that he, and other American Catholics like him, are not really proper Catholics in this one area of their thought. While it is important that American Protestants display an increasing maturity of judgment on this matter, it is also important that Roman Catholicism do all it can to correct what many of us hope is a false understanding of itself. It is a matter of relief to the Protestant that this is an area in which no *de fide* pronouncements have been made, and in which there is consequently still room for the healthiest kind of Catholic discussion and opposition to the "thesis-hypothesis" view.

Consequently, I do not think there is a single matter on which more good could be done in terms of the relationship between Roman Catholicism and Protestantism, than by some authoritative message from the council about toleration and religious liberty.

II

A second area in which the non-Catholic would appreciate help from the Second Vatican Council does concern an already existing *de fide* pronouncement, and the one, indeed, which is the single greatest source of difficulty. The First Vatican Council, as we are all aware, forthrightly defined the dogma of papal infallibility. Nothing could seem more explicit on first examination, particularly in the light of the careful way in which the definition was set forth. And yet, the further one tries to understand it, the less confident he is, either that he himself understands it, or even that the Catholic Church has said its final word on the matter.

This proceeds in part from the fact—so baffling to the non-Catholic —that nobody seems to be quite sure just what are and what are not the distinctively infallible utterances. This has the unfortunate result that the only affirmation about which there can be absolutely no doubt as to its infallible status is the Dogma of the Assumption—the very dogma which is farthest away doctrinally from the Protestant understanding of the New Testament gospel.

But such matters have been dealt with at great length in other situations. What is needed from the Second Vatican Council is an amplification of the definition of the First Vatica Council. What, for example, is the relationship of the infallibility of the pope, the chief bishop, to the other bishops, all of whom have responsibility for setting forth the true Catholic faith? More basic: where, precisely, does infallibility inhere? The usual answer is that of course it inheres in the pope himself. The inference is drawn from the last words of the Vatican Decree, that the "definitions of the Roman Pontiff are irreformable of themselves, and not from the consent of the Church (. . . *ex sese, non autem ex consensu Ecclesiae*)." But I have discovered strong opposition among Catholics themselves to the notion that the Vatican Council gave an individual power to proclaim dogmas that might derive elsewhere than from the consent of the Church. It is urged by them that infallibility really inheres *in the Church,* and that the pope only serves as the means by which the faith of the Church is articulated. This emphasis is based on an earlier phrase in the definition, which speaks of the Roman Pontiff's being "possessed of that infallibility with which the divine Redeemer willed that *his Church* should be endowed (. . . *ea infallibilitate pollere, qua divinus Redemptor Ecclesiam suam . . . esse voluit*)."

The difference may seem a subtle one. Perhaps it is. But it is one of those subtleties the implications of which are of the most far-reaching sort. If infallibility inheres essentially in the Church, for whom the pope is the mouthpiece, then this means, for example, that the breach between Catholicism and Eastern Orthodoxy may not be as unbridgeable as it once seemed. It may not noticeably lessen the gap between Catholicism and Protestantism, but it at least states the terms of difficulty somewhat differently.

But the present concern is not to argue the differences and assess the implications of two different interpretations. The present concern is merely to underline the fact that obviously the last word has not been spoken by the Roman Church on the meaning of infallibility, and that confusions concerning it are apparent not only outside the Roman communion but evidently within it also. It will be a great service to all concerned, therefore, if the Second Vatican Council can, in a sense, begin where the First Vatican Council concluded, by expanding the minimal terms thus far at our disposal concerning the meaning of infallibility.

Let me comment briefly on one further dimension of this problem of infallibility. A favorite Protestant slogan is *ecclesia reformata sed semper reformanda.* We often use it to distinguish our Protestant heritage from that of Roman Catholicism, which, endowed with infallibility, claims not to need reformation. I think the distinction is true enough as far as it goes, but I am not as sure as I once was that it goes very far. I believe Visser 't Hooft was right when he pointed out that Roman Catholicism can contemplate reforms *in* the church, but never reform *of* the church. Nevertheless, Protestants often jump to the conclusion that Roman Catholicism cannot acknowledge any need of reform. This, of course, is patently untrue. But it is never very clear *to what degree* the principle of reformation can operate within Roman Catholicism. When Catholic writers themselves use the phrase *ecclesia semper reformanda,* as they do increasingly these days, just what do they mean by it? Do they mean anything more than cleaning up certain peripheral matters that have now become anachronistic? It is not at all clear to the Protestant just how infallibility and *semper reformanda* are related to one another. Perhaps it is impossible to state the relationship in a way that the Protestant can really understand. I hope an attempt will be made. But even if it is not, the increasing acknowledgement of the need for reform on the part of the Catholic Church itself is a hopeful sign to Protestant observers.

III

My third concern has to do with the teaching office of the Church, and is a request that the Council concern itself with the moral issues of greatest moment to twentieth century man: nuclear war and racial discrimination. Not only the rest of Christendom, but the rest of mankind, is concerned for clearer light on both of these matters. On the first of these, nuclear war, the "Christian position" is far from clear, and to the degree that the Council can help to clarify it, it will find itself speaking the most relevant word it could possibly speak. By contrast, on the second matter, that of racial discrimination, the Christian position is very clear, but it has been so ineptly voiced in Christian circles that it is infrequently practiced. The reluctance of the various branches of Christendom, whether Protestant or Catholic, to *act* within their own lives, upon the basis of the clear teaching of the gospel about race, is not only a great moral blot upon their ministry to twentieth century man, but a major reason why men do not turn to the churches with more hope of finding within them the truth men so desperately seek. Unless the church can speak with more clarity and precision on the matter of race, where its gospel is clear, it will forfeit the right to speak on such issues as nuclear war, where its gospel still seems far from clear. Here it is a source of disappointment, particularly on the American scene, that the otherwise admirable encyclical, *Mater et magistra,* did not, in dealing with contemporary social problems, give special attention to the moral and ethical implications of the race problem. And since this is not a matter confined to the United States, but an area of tension and explosive conflict in all parts of the world, we must hope for forthright statements from the Roman Church, both by the Second Vatican Council and also in later encyclicals. We need an encyclical as clear and explicit on the race question as *Mit Brennender Sorge* was on the Nazi question.

In whatever comments it may make about nuclear war, we have no right to demand that the Second Ecumenical Council come up with a formula for preventing World War III. But the resources of Catholic faith and history need to be brought to bear upon the problem in both conciliar and papal statements. There are certainly aspects of the traditional "just war" doctrine that need re-thinking in the light of nuclear weapons. That such re-thinking is not yet complete may be urged by some as a reason for saying that the time is not yet ripe for any definite statements. But time is a commodity all too precious if World War III is to be avoided, and if any church enjoys too long the luxury of contemplation it may discover that there is no world left to contemplate.

In America today, a violent brand of anti-Communism (which a few voices in the American Catholic Church have helped to foster) is being wedded to a kind of self-righteous Americanist nationalism. The combination of these two ingredients may very easily create a third, namely a psychological viewpoint that is susceptible to the validity of the concept of "preventive war." In the face of such a disastrous possibility, it is of utmost importance that the Catholic Church make common cause with all men who seek ways of checking inflamed national pride and of dealing responsibly with the infinitely perplexing moral dilemma of living in a nuclear age.

IV

There is one other area in which the Council could clarify the present thinking of the Roman Catholic Church. This concerns the Catholic understanding of the laity. There is an ultimate division between Catholics and Protestants on the nature of the relationship of clergy and laity. The Catholic usually interprets the Protestant concern with "the priesthood of all believers" as though it really meant "the priesthood of no believers," i.e., as an assertion that there are no real priests in the Protestant understanding of the matter. And the Protestant, in his turn, usually interprets the Catholic emphasis upon the priesthood as though it meant that the laity do not really count. What is involved here is not simply a matter of getting a better understanding of one another's positions, although that would certainly help, and would make it possible for Catholics to understand that Protestants were trying to elevate laity into priesthood rather than devalue priests into laymen, and for Protestants to understand that Catholics see the role of the laity as an essential one in "the communion of saints." Here is an area, however, where there is need to go beyond past misunderstandings of past formulas, to renewed appreciation of the fresh thinking that is proceeding on both sides.

Immense good can be done by the Council if it will articulate, in a more official way, the status of some of the currents of thought that are at present directed to a fresh theological understanding of the laity. Fr. Congar's *Lay People in the Church* is an example of this strand of Catholic thought. The emphasis in so much recent Catholic writing on "the apostolate of the laity" is another. Furthermore, the gradual emergence on the American scene of articulate Catholic lay spokesmen also makes desirable some clearer accounting of just for whom, and how significantly, they can be said to speak. There is a tendency on the part of American non-Catholics to discount the utterances of American Catholic laymen by some such comment as, "Oh, he's only a layman," with the corresponding implication that his voice doesn't count.

When I hear Catholic theologians willing to begin a discussion of priesthood with a firm acceptance of "the priesthood of all believers," I do not conclude that they are about to become Protestants, but I do conclude that such statements indicate areas of possible *rapprochement* that were not available a few decades ago. And I, along with other American Protestants, await more light from the Roman Catholic side, as to just how far such *rapprochement* is likely to go.

V

Let me reiterate in conclusion what I tried to suggest at the beginning. It has been no part of my intention to suggest that the Second Vatican Council must become "more Protestant" if the Protestant is to be encouraged by its proceedings. Such a request would be not only unreasonable but unrealistic. It *is* proper to suggest, however, that the real purpose of the Second Vatican Council is to be *truly catholic,* and this concern lies behind the suggestions in the pages above. If the Second Vatican Council is truly catholic, it will give immense help not only to those of its own flock, but to those outside as well.

Roger Schutz

Our Serene Hope

*B*efore answering the questions that have been posed, I wish to make known my deepest desire not to bring judgment on the institutions of the Roman Church, which I love, for I see in her the Body of Our Lord Jesus Christ.

Nothing is easier than to judge from the outside. But I am a man who stands outside. If I assumed the authority to judge, I would be a source of scandal, and would have understood nothing of the great difficulties surrounding the quest for Christian unity.

It is only in a spirit of humility that I can answer these questions. This humility is proper because I am conscious of carrying within my very being the seed of divisiveness, in opposition to the visible unity of all Christians in one Church.

My answer will not be a personal one. I will strive (in general terms) to express what seems to me to come from the depths of the Protestant conscience.

I. What Importance Does the Council Have With Respect to the Reconciliation of the Christian Churches and the Mission of the Church?

The search for unity among Christians demands infinite prudence and careful preparations. Nevertheless, by the calling of a Council, an impetus has been given which cannot help but hasten developments. This act seems to constitute a providential ecumenical stimulant. It has created among the Protestant laity throughout the world a tremendous sense of hope. It has reawakened in them an ecumenical consciousness that was slumbering.

The preparation for the Council among Catholics and the spirit of hope among Protestants creates very favorable conditions for the visible unity of all Christians. It is being discovered that unity is not an end

Roger Schutz is prior of the Taizé Community. His book, Living Today for God *was brought out by Helicon this spring.*

The Taizé Community is one of the most important centers in the work for Christian unity. It also represents a creative response to the monastic vocation within contemporary Protestantism.

revival; a reform and simplification of divine services is long overdue. The ancient liturgy is deserving of respect, but pride in our lineage is less important in this area than recapturing a spirit of youth and doing everything possible to make the inner meaning of the liturgy more available to the spiritually hungry masses of our day. The penitential discipline of the Church might also be examined from the same point of view. It needs refocusing and re-orientation. In many places the confessional has become an absolution-machine. Homiletics can be taught more seriously, and the new spirit of biblical homiletics should be given strong encouragement. Scripture services and bible vigils, which have been tried out in France and Belgium—and to a lesser extent, in the United States—deserve to be imitated in the whole Church. Another suggestion worthy of consideration is the distribution of communion under both species on certain occasions. This practice would appear to be feasible at retreats and other occasions when the congregations are small enough so that the service will be dignified.

An effort at clarification would be welcome in regard to the doctrine of purgatory. The Church has never defined purgatory as a place of fire. It should be taught as a state of purification in the most spiritual sense, without the gory detail that is now being preached and read in so many prayer books. The Council of Trent was very wise to guarantee only the fact that a purgatory exists and that we can help the souls in purgatory. That is all that was ever said on the basis of the infallibility of the Church.

Freedom in liturgical development from nation to nation would be a great encouragement to the new nations that are entering the Church in Africa and Asia. We have today enough scholars in Europe and America to take care of the historical and pastoral side of the needed liturgical reform, but it will seriously impede the gain that might be expected from this movement in the lives of the faithful if we remain Latin-speaking, at least in those parts of the Mass which require the participation and understanding of the people. It would also be unfortunate if an exaggerated insistence on Latin obscured the degree, through the liturgy, to which we share a common patrimony with the Orthodox, and to some extent, with England and some of the Lutheran countries.

A relevant preaching on poverty, particularly in the countries of greater affluence, is sorely needed. In keeping with such preaching, the style of life of the shepherd should be in conformity with the poor of his flock; it is hard to understand a pastor who drives around in a Cadillac while he has families in his parish that cannot pay their doctor bills. Surely, no priest wishes to live ostentatiously; the problem is to insure that the economic level of the priest should not exceed that of his average parishioner.

As far as question number 3 is concerned, it is important to keep in mind that although the Council is a legislative body which can make

Theological Factors:

(a) They are looking forward to a clarification of the relationship of authority among the Pope, the bishops and the Council; they hope especially that the dogma of papal infallibility will be made more explicit with respect to its meaning both for the Council and for the whole Church.

(b) They hope that Mariology will be placed in a clearer relationship to Christology, that the former will be more enlightened by the latter, and, above all, that further definitions will be postponed which might deepen the gap between us. Some manifestations of Marian piety might lead one to believe that there is a certain laxity on the part of some theologians.

Non-Theological Factors:

(a) These Protestants are aware that the temporal possessions of certain Protestant sects weigh heavily upon them, to the point of being a stumbling-block for the indifferent. Just as they deplore an unavowed need for temporal power that is manifest in some of their institutions, these Protestants hope that the Catholic Church, too, will appear more and more as first and foremost the Church of those without power in this world, the oppressed and the hungry. In fact, the Virgin Mary was able to proclaim that through the coming of Christ the weak would be made strong and the mighty brought low.

It would seem that the wealth of the Catholic Church is more apparent than real. But if this temporal power or wealth is only a façade, those Protestants who love the Church ask if it would not be better to sacrifice such a façade. Nevertheless, these Protestants know that the service of the Church requires tangible means for its work, a whole visible apparatus, at once considerable in its proportions and indispensable. Therefore, their reactions come, not from a spirit of puritanism, but simply from the desire to expel from the minds of their own brethren a criticism which is now four centuries old.

In this context, the gift by the Brazilian Bishops of vast estates which were possessions of the Church is truly significant. Some of the very natural and simple actions of Pope John evoke an equally sympathetic reaction.

(b) Finally, these favorably inclined Protestants fear that the Council will speak of the "return" of the separated brethren. It is clear that this expression grates on Protestants. It gives the impression that the Church is awaiting unconditional surrender on the part of Protestants. The expression "return" is far removed from the thinking of the man of today, who prefers to surpass himself as he proceeds on his march forward.

3. How do We Protestants Experience the Expectation of Unity?

While it reawakened ecumenical sensibility in the whole Catholic Church, the calling of the Council stirred up real hope among those Protestants working for unity. Protestants notice among many Catholics a serious interest in their separated brethren, and in itself this is something new. The expectation of unity is so alive in a great part of the Catholic Church that it cannot help but arouse in us a fervent patience. It is important that we should do nothing to frustrate such expectations and to adopt the spirit of hope that we sense among Catholics.

For Protestants this means a spirit of purification and a non-parochial attitude. In fact, in the work toward Christian unity, there are preliminary conditions to be established whose outlines are already taking shape: viz., to abandon the notion of considering division of Christians as normal or inevitable; to learn to see one's Christian neighbor with the glance of Christ Himself; to see Christ in others, that is to say, the best of what God has placed in men. As a Protestant, I must remember that the sin of my Catholic brother is a matter for God and his confessor; and I must prepare myself spiritually to understand that the union of Christians will not be the triumph of one group over another. If there were to be victory for one side and defeat for the other, no one would be willing to accept such a unity.

Thus we prepare ourselves for a purification, for a certain type of death to the self, for a renunciation of all that is not essential and necessary to the proclamation of truth in the world. So many non-theological factors, traditions of secondary importance, and even matters of peripheral practice, continue to separate us. Certainly, we must not minimize the importance of the truth, the affirmation of major dogmatic positions; but if only these real problems separated us, we would be far closer than anyone would suspect—and let us never stop affirming this to be true.

What shall we expect from the Council? In any case, new paths have been opened which shall not be closed.

Will conclusive events take place? Perhaps. We believe that the Holy Spirit will speak to the Council. Thus an event can occur which will profoundly enlighten all Christians. Nevertheless, even if such a happening, which might take place within the institution of the Church, should not be apparent to our eyes, the Council will remain in itself an event of the divine order.

That spirit which consists in expecting nothing for fear of being disappointed is not in accord with God. Without the hope of faith, without a living assurance that God acts, we can no longer advance toward God, and on the ecumenical plane our vocation would be snuffed out.

Let us rejoice that the Catholic conscience, in particular, has become open to the ecumenical spirit through the fact of preparing for the

Council. It is incumbent upon us as Protestants to sustain this surge, to nurture the flame, to experience the suffering attendant upon division within the depths of our souls in secret union with Christ.

Thus, after so long a separation, we can learn again that in our days God visits us and showers us with his gifts, provided we stand before Him, thanking Him for His gift of the present, refusing to look back to our past divisions, not even to that day that was yesterday.

translated by GEORGE E. GINGRAS

VORAVUT CHANYAVANICH (Thailand), CLAUDE
CHIANG (China), RONALD D'COSTA (India), AL-
BERT KABANGA (Rhodesia), IGNACE KARUHIJE
(Ruanda), THOMAS MIZUNAMI (Japan), ANNIE
NARIKUZHY (India), NGUYEN THI THANH TUYEN
(Vietnam), JOSEPH OEI HAK LIANG (Indonesia),
RAMON C. REYES (Philippines), RIM TJYONG-HUN
(Korea), THEOPHILE YOU (Korea)

Asian and African Laymen and the Council

This is not a formal statement by theologians, nor a systematic study.
It is not even a presentation of our requests for consideration by the
Fathers of the Council. We have no intention of telling our bishops what
they ought to do, either at the Council or in our countries. This text
is simply the resumé of a completely free and spontaneous discussion
which was held among Catholic Students with regard to the Council.
We emphasize that it was "à propos" the Council since we do not know
exactly which, among the subjects which we took up, are matters for
discussion at a Council and which only concern the ordinary life of
the Church. But the climate that has been created by the preparation
of the Council gives us a livelier sense of what seems good to us, and
what seems less good. We will speak both of what we regret to see in
the Church, and of what we hope for from it and from our Christian
brothers, especially in the Asian and African countries where we were
born and to which we will soon return.

At the moment we are in Europe pursuing university studies. This
opportunity has allowed us to become familiar with aspects and experiences of Christianity that we might not have known if we had remained
in our countries. Has this modified our point of view on the life of the

*As the text makes clear, this article is a report, based on a discussion held at
the Maison Saint-Jean of Louvain University, Belgium, among a dozen university students from various Asian and African countries. It appeared to be
a useful supplement to the exclusively "western" preoccupations of the Catholic participants to this issue's symposium, and we are grateful to the outstanding mission bi-monthly, EGLISE VIVANTE (61, Blvd. Schreurs, Louvain, Belgium,
$4) for allowing us to translate it from the March 1962 issue.*

Church? Possibly. This situation has encouraged our taking stock of certain problems and has put us in the position of formulating our feelings more clearly. But we are not pretending to represent anyone in this statement; each of us has spoken exclusively for himself. Even when it is said that "in our country" Christians think or wish such-and-such, this only means that we think we understand what they think or desire. We have made no inquiry, and we are not attempting to provide a scientifically objective presentation of the situation. It seemed interesting to us, both for ourselves and perhaps also for the Church, to express what we felt, sincerely, frankly and clearly, out of the love that we bear to our faith, the Church, and our peoples.

Perhaps it would have been better if we had reproduced our discussion exactly as it took place, in all its spontaneity. But this would have made it quite long and probably quite disorganized. We have thought it preferable to organize our reflections in a certain order, and in the form of a report which would express them as faithfully as possible.

Are We Concerned?

What have we done for the Council since the time it was announced? We have prayed, certainly, but is that enough? Several of us took part last year in the study conference organized by the Overseas Students Coordination.[1] At that time the Council was discussed and someone suggested the idea that each of us write personally to our bishop in order to let him know what we thought on the subject of the Council. In practice, none of us decided to do this. One of us thought that it would show a lack of respect, and give the appearance of wanting to advise the bishop, without having been invited to do so; after all, his point of view might well be justified by reasons of which we are unaware. Rightly or wrongly, we thought that a letter written by a single layman had no chance of being taken into consideration and none of us felt like writing just for the exercise. Possibly we were wrong in not writing our bishops, but our pessimism in regard to the chance of being heard in any serious sense may in itself also be relevant to the situation. Does it not suggest a distance which in fact has been built up between Catholics and their pastors? Without wishing to assign responsibility or generalize too widely, is it not profoundly regrettable that laymen feel so removed from their bishop that they end up believing that it is useless to address themselves to him?

Although this desire to write is sterile, it shows nevertheless that those who experience it feel personally concerned about the coming Council. It seems to us that this attitude is far from general. The vast majority of

---

1 This is a coordinating organization for African, Asian and Caribbean Catholic students in Europe.

laymen understand that they are asked to pray, but otherwise, in their minds a Council is the business of bishops. In a sense, this is true. The great problems involving Christian unity, the relations between the papacy and the episcopacy, etc., which are discussed in theological terms in publications on the preparation of the Council, obviously can be studied and resolved only by our bishops and their theologians. The manner in which they are generally presented reinforces the impression that all this is only of quite indirect interest to laymen. In order for them to feel genuinely concerned, they must first have understood that, beyond these problems, it is the whole renewal of the Church, and hence of their own Christian habits, which is at stake. Especially when it is a question of our countries and our people, they must understand that the Council will inevitably be the occasion of a great change in the development of our young churches and their place in the universal Church.

The Dialogue with our Cultures

The most fundamental question that is posed to the Church in our countries is certainly that of its practical aptitude to encounter our national cultures in a profound manner. As things now stand, if we want something authentic from the cultural point of view, in the majority of cases we have to look for it outside the Christian community.

At the last world Eucharistic Congress in Munich (1960), a great success was scored in the beautiful and valid performance of Indian dances which celebrated the Holy Sacrament. In order to execute this suggestion of a missionary, however, it was necessary to get the help of a non-Christian choreographer. The Christian ideas had to be explained to her, and then she knew how to give them an authentic Indian expression. A Catholic found it very difficult to find the right note, to discern what could and what could not be transposed from Hinduism to Christianity, without shocking Hindus and distorting the Christian faith. The fact is that national culture and Christian faith are not integrated in the life of Catholics.

This is a general difficulty in Asian and African nations. Earlier generations of Christians perhaps had a less lively sense of this, because they lived in a period of cultural alienation. Those of us who were born in the Catholic community are more or less accustomed to it. On the other hand, a number of relatively recent converts declare that they have been "astonished" to see the incapacity of the Church to adopt, even while Christianizing them, the valid expressions of the soul of their people.

Let us be well understood; it is not some little "adaptations" which interest us. These can be good, and can also be ambiguous. They are only valuable if they are seen as the normal expression of a profound attitude. Our Indian friends presented some examples which seem characteristic of the situation in many of our countries. Indians are flattered when they see foreigners live in the Indian style and will feel greater sympathy for them for this reason, but they will have only ridicule for their Catholic fellow-citizens who, after being educated in western ways, suddenly assume an archaic mode of life and begin to wear traditional Hindu clothes. At the Marian congress in Bombay (1954), images of the Virgin in Indian style gave rise to mixed comments, and some even accused Catholics of having attempted this "adaptation" out of opportunism, to please the government. On the other hand, everyone praised the fact that prominent non-Christian personalities were invited to the congress. The "Indian" representation of the Virgin is an attempt, whether skillful or awkward, to affirm oneself as Indian in unilateral fashion; the sympathetic presence of non-Christians at our side bears witness to a desire for dialogue, openness and mutual comprehension, which seem far more urgent than the sari of the Virgin who, in fact, never wore one and is nonetheless our universal mother.

The Church will, eventually, be effectively "adapted"—or better, "integrated"—in our countries. In order to achieve this, however, it is immediately necessary, above all, that it be adaptable. It will be able to demonstrate this capacity to the degree in which its representatives will know how to understand, accept and love the various peoples of the world *just as they are.* In Europe too, every country and every human milieu needs to be understood, accepted and loved just as it is; the same nourishment must be prepared differently for a child, an adult, and an old man. We make all kinds of serious errors when we do not see the man with whom we wish to communicate *as he is.* It is quite a different thing to preach the gospel to someone who, without being Christian, is nevertheless deeply religious, than simply to address "unbelievers." To include both in the same category of preaching "to pagans" is simply not meeting men as they are. In the same way, the current tendency to translate everything into terms of under-development is dangerous; it may help in arousing sentiments of pity and a certain dynamism in aiding the needy, but we risk forgetting that beneath his rags the "underdeveloped" man may conceal the nobility of a soul more attracted by spiritual values than by material goods.

Has the Christian mission taken sufficiently into account the religious values of those people it has evangelized? If it has not, can we say that it has encountered these men as they really are?

A serious dialogue with cultures, and the religions which are their soul, appears to us as an urgent task, if we wish to achieve the indispensable integration of the Church and our peoples.

The Adaptability of the Church

We are all convinced of the Church's desire to see this integration take place. What appears to be the question is the adaptability that this integration postulates in the formulation of doctrine and the manifestations of Christian life. We are sometimes brought to ask ourselves in sadness if those who in effect represent the Church in our countries will succeed in rediscovering this indispensable flexibility. We would wish our bishops, both national and foreign, would tell us clearly if they see a genuine possibility in the near future of softening the current rigidity of ecclesiastical behavior. In saying this, again we are not thinking of minor secondary matters, but of important changes, for example, in the presentation of dogma. Of course, dogmatic truth cannot change, but the question is precisely whether we do not often extend this immutability to things which in fact only relate to the explanation and presentation of dogma. One of us gave the Eucharist as an example, asking himself if it were absolutely unalterable that the matter of the sacrament be bread and wine, which were so expressive in Christ's country, but so alien to the Far East. This is only an example. Perhaps it will alarm some theologians and we do not wish to insist on the particular point; it is mentioned only because it makes clear that our questions in regard to "adaptability" have wide implications and would require theologians to make an effort to state precisely what can be modified and what is immutable. It is not a question of attitudes in regard to the day-to-day pastoral effort, which can be left to practical psychology and to the good sense of pastors. We are dealing with a fundamental problem, which is very close to the domain of faith; that is why it seems to us that it should receive the attention of the Council. Indeed, if it is absolutely necessary to proceed by way of categories developed by the western mind, how will our peoples ever be able to feel that they are at home in Christianity? And how will Christianity ever find expression in a manner adequate to the proper genius of our cultures?

We understand very well that we are dealing with an extremely complex and delicate problem. But it seems to us that everything else depends on it; if we are to be sincere, we cannot conceal the anxiety that we feel, perhaps along with a degree of youthful impatience, at the delay in translating into reality those declarations of principle that have been so clearly and frequently made by the popes. These statements repeatedly stress the compatibility of Christianity with the genuine values found in all human cultures, and the freedom of Christianity in relation to every particular culture, and most notably, in relation to the West.

A Liturgy that Would Speak to Us

Fortunately, there are simpler questions, for which satisfactory responses can probably be given without great difficulty.

Among other matters, we are thinking of liturgy. It brings the Christian people to hear the Word of God, it expresses the whole Christian mystery in gestures, attitudes, and symbols. But how would the Christian people really be able to *hear* this Word of God when it is given to them in translation, in a foreign language? In our countries, among workers and peasants, and even for many intellectuals, Latin will always remain a foreign language. The Church's decision to use Latin for theology, and even as the "clerical" language, can certainly be justified, but we do not understand why the vernacular is not also employed in the catechetical parts of the Mass, if we want these prayers to achieve their purpose. As regards gestures, attitudes and symbols, it seems to us that the adaptability of which we spoke before should allow us to adapt them, at least to some degree, to our own sensibilities and traditions.

Why should we "give the peace" to our brothers by a kiss which is distasteful to our customs and cannot have any spiritual resonance in the context of our countries? Why should it not be possible for the office of the dead to be celebrated in white vestments in that part of the world where this color is universally understood as the equivalent of black in the West? Would it be less expressive of the Christian meaning of death which leads to beatitude and resurrection? Examples could be multiplied. They have been given on many occasions, and for a long time. What are we waiting for in order to move ahead?

In the course of our discussion, one of our group remarked judiciously that the sacred is necessarily different from the secular, and that an unconsidered change of symbols might result in a liturgy which replaced the sacred with the secular. In fact, this is a danger. But is it enough for something to be incomprehensible in order for it to be assured of being understood as sacred?

"When I was still a Protestant," another remarked, "I entered by chance into various Catholic churches of my province. It was with astonishment that I watched ceremonies in which it was impossible for me to understand anything. With the Protestants, on the other hand, I was able to follow the development of the service and to understand something about Christianity. If I had not come to Europe, I doubt that I would ever have become a Catholic.

Nevertheless, we have many fervent Catholics in our countries. They have always been accustomed to this "far-away" liturgy, an affair of priests, which they accept as such without posing questions for themselves. But is this the ideal of the Christian liturgy? The renewal that it manifests elsewhere shows that one is right to expect more of it. For this, however, it is necessary that it again become something alive, speaking to men about God in their own language and sensibility. In our churches there remains a great deal yet to do in this direction.

The Scandal of the Weak

If everything that we have been saying up till now gives the impression that we are revolutionaries, this report would betray the character of our discussions, which constantly emphasized the imperative necessity of great prudence in every evolution of Christian concerns. We are completely of the opinion that no change, even minimal, should be introduced in the customary habits of the Catholics of our countries unless minds have been carefully prepared for it. The meaning of the change ought to be clearly explained, and at some length, in order that it be correctly interpreted by the faithful. Otherwise, we will often give occasion for scandal, and create the impression that religion "changes."

This remark has been made in all areas, but is especially justified in our Christian communities because they are comparatively young. Ordinary Catholics have been accustomed to put everything on the same level: faith in the Eucharist and devotion to the Sacred Heart, the episcopacy and the shape of the mitre, the use of Latin, the priesthood and wearing a cassock. In the popular mind, all this is included under the same heading as the patrimony of the positive values of the Church. They have been told so often that the use of Latin expresses the universality of Catholicism and distinguishes it from Protestantism, that they would suspect that their parish priest was turning Protestant if he read them the epistle in their own language. This effect of scandal has recently been produced by the modification of the Eucharistic fast.

Opposition to change is not so great in all our countries. There are also differences between older Catholics and recent converts. On the whole, however, our missionary churches are extremely traditional.

It appears important to us, therefore, that the teaching of religion be more exact and painstaking, giving more emphasis to a certain hierarchy of spiritual values. The attitude that "everything we do here is good, everything is bad elsewhere," is a handy simplification, but it betrays the truth. The Church will not be diminished by saying that a given practice is secondary, and can be modified according to times and places.

At the beginning of evangelization, perhaps it was necessary to simplify the teaching to an extreme degree. Today there is an increasing percentage of the faithful who have completed not only primary but secondary school; can we not profit by this rise in the general level of instruction in order to bring religious teaching up-to-date?

In our opinion there are now enough laymen open to changes to support the action of the clergy, and to aid them in making its true meaning understood by all. An excess of prudence must not result in the disaffection of the most serious Christians, under pretext of protecting the others.

Our Clergy

The orientations of which we have spoken and the education of the faithful that they presupposed led us to speak of our priests, both those born among our people and those that have come from foreign lands.

In his missionary encyclical *Princeps Pastorum*, John XXIII deals at some length with the formation of a missionary clergy. We do not have the competence to say what it ought to be. We would simply like to remark that this formation conditions the whole life of our Christian communities. We would also like to say that, among the encyclical's directives, we especially appreciated the insistence of the pope on a serious missiological preparation which is "careful to form the judgment of priests on local cultural values, especially philosophical and religious ones, and their relation to the Christian religion." We have the impression, however, that some delays in the necessary evolution are to be explained by the clergy's fear of committing errors, a fear due in great part to a lack of adequate preparation. A clergy of open spirit, having the sense of all its responsibilities and not afraid of initiatives, intellectually equipped to act because of its knowledge of the situation—that is, the clergy that the encyclical describes—such is the indispensable guide which our churches need in order to develop and integrate themselves into the Asian and African world.

We cannot help but have the impression that, because of the formation that they have generally received until now, our local clergy is unintentionally oriented towards the imitation of the West rather than to our own cultures. Doubtless, this was an inevitable stage of development, but we would very much like to see it surmounted.

A clergy that was formed in the spirit of the pontifical directives would be quickly and easily in agreement on the initiatives to adopt. And its unanimity would be a very important element in overcoming the resistance of "traditionalists" and inspiring the faithful with confidence. The simplicity, modesty, and warm benevolence shown by our Holy Father have helped to produce a new climate in the Church, and provide the best example of the type of pastor we would wish to see everywhere.

The Role of the Laity

Naturally, the discussion of our own responsibilities as Christian laymen was not absent from our debates. We did not try to study the layman as such, but to situate his function in the over-all life of the Church, as we see it in actual circumstances. We were concerned, first, with the role of laymen in the Christian community, then in relation to non-Christians, and finally, in the life of the nation.

As laymen, that is, as members of the people of God, we believe we have the duty to speak, if we happen to become aware of something in the Church which disturbs us, or which we do not understand. We do not pretend to be always right. If we think that sometimes we are in a position to enlighten our pastors, it is not directly as regards what path is to be followed, but as to the reactions of the Christian people of which we are part. We only desire to help priests in their awesome responsibilities as spiritual guides. We believe we can and ought to help them become better acquainted with the aspirations and reactions of their flock. We also believe we can and ought to help them make their intentions better understood to our fellow laymen. Our wish is to see our priests accept our help and place their confidence in us as regards those areas in which we can be positively active as Catholics.

Our position as laymen gives us more opportunity to make contact with non-Christians, especially in the perspective mentioned earlier of a dialogue with non-Christian religions. In order that such a dialogue be fruitful, it is first necessary that laymen be specially prepared for it, and then that their action should be seen not simply as a personal intervention, but as an integral part of the action of the Church. Is it impossible for lay groups to be formed and given a mandate for an apostolate of this kind?

Perhaps this suggestion is premature, coming from our group, since in our countries Catholic Action itself is still very tightly controlled by the clergy. In the majority of cases the laymen has been only a figurehead, without genuine responsibility. Besides, it must be recognized that since he is accustomed to receive his entire orientation from the clergy, he is not prepared for his mission. We feel this very strongly when we meet Protestant fellow-citizens, who are better prepared in this regard than we are.

"It is necessary to specify more precisely the limits of infallibility," one of us remarked humorously. He did not intend his phrase to be understood in the way it is employed by theologians who are working on preparatory commissions for the Council. He was thinking of that infallibility, we might call it, which certain priests believe they enjoy in the most varied areas, sometimes including the most obviously secular concerns. Perhaps the Council will give us further teaching on the layman and his role in the life of the Church; this would surely offer an efficacious remedy for that clericalism from which too many of our Christian communities still suffer.

This clericalism is partly explained in our countries by the practical necessity in which many priests, at the beginnings of evangelization, were obliged to assume all the burdens themselves. But the progress of this evangelization should permit a division of activities which would leave to the layman what belongs to his own domain, and thus achieve greater efficiency.

At present the situation is such that some of us confess that when they return to their country they will not dare to take the initiatives which appear legitimate and desirable to them, for fear of being singled out as unreliable, and thus causing more harm than good. Even though we hope that such pessimism is exaggerated, we ought to recognize that such a situation is stultifying.

There would be a great deal to say on the subject of our role in public life. Religious life and human life have for us too often constituted separate areas. Either the Catholic keeps aloof from the work of national development, or his devotion to it is expressed through activity in which his Christian spirit exercises almost no influence. The Christian vocation to the *res publica* seems to us not to have the place which it merits in the missionary perspective.

Aftermath of the Colonial Age

A good number of the deficiencies from which Christian life suffers in our countries are at least partially explained by the situation which was the result of history. It is a fact that most of our countries are just now emerging from the colonial era. The consequences of this heritage are not magically eliminated by the proclamation of independence.

In many former colonies, it is difficult to forget that the missionaries belonged to the colonizing power, and their establishment took place concurrently with that of the foreign regime. Even we Catholics cannot completely forget this, and we feel it is even harder for our non-Catholic fellow-citizens to forget it. This creates a malaise which destroys confidence, and to some degree causes that regrettable divorce between the public and religious life of Catholics which we have mentioned.

Problems must be faced squarely, and then solutions can be sought. Time is doubtless on our side, but its action must be given direction. Besides, the speed of the world's evolution today does not permit us simply to wait until time has done its work.

Relations between Churches

If we have left the question of the relations between Christians belonging to different Churches for the last, this is not because we give less importance to it. But if there is one area where a sudden shift of attitude is certain to cause scandal, it is this. For too long and with too much insistence the teaching that we have received on the subject of Protestantism has been nothing but a fiercely defensive apologetics. Many of the Catholics in our countries see Protestants only as candidates for hell. The mentality of the average Catholic in our areas is so backward in this regard that it is impossible to speak now without scandal of a reconciliation of any scope.

As far as we are concerned, however, it is this situation which scandalizes us. Although we recognize that pastoral prudence forbids too sudden an about-face, we do not understand why preaching on the subject of Protestants should not develop a more ecumenical spirit. Besides, negative criticism is not even a sensible approach. Life today creates so many human contacts between Christian laymen of all confessions that exaggeration and injustice is easily recognized. Ultimately, the negative approach runs the risk of back-firing against the preacher, leaving the layman without any valid information on which to base judgments on the various ways of being Christian.

It appears indispensable and urgent to us, therefore, that our priests gradually change the spirit of their teaching on Protestantism, and try to establish contacts with pastors, which can have so much constructive value. These things appear to us to be required both by that fraternal charity which should rule all relations between Christians, and by the demands of missionary action in our countries.

Conclusion

Let us return to the Council, which was the occasion of our discussion. We realize very well that it will not immediately remedy all deficiencies, and could not realize all desirable readjustments in a single act. Moreover, we also know, perhaps without saying enough about it, that changes are already being effected and initiatives taken in many places without waiting for the Council. But our hope is that this general assembly of bishops will affirm an orientation, and raise to the level of the Church's official attitude a number of actions taken on a local and unofficial, sometimes even an individual basis. In this way a climate of renewal will be created which the very preparation of the Council has helped us begin to breathe.

Much has been said of a probable decentralization of the administrative powers of the Church. It seems to us that this would assist in the integration of our cultures and peoples, since it would allow the bishops to take useful measures quickly and on the spot.

As we bring this report to a close, we wish to say again that if sometimes it has seemed to adopt a critical tone, this is only through our awkwardness in expressing our desires. Because we love the Church, we want it to be more beautiful every day, more holy, and more explicitly universal.

translated by JOSEPH E. CUNNEEN

Augustine Cardinal Bea

The Council and Christian Unity

Introduction

*I*t is a special joy for me to speak to you on the theme, "The Council and Christian Unity," and to treat of this subject before such a select audience, in view of the fact that the day is not far off when the Holy Father will convoke the great assembly that is due to meet this very year.

Although this Council will not be, as we know, a "Council of Union," it will also "be profitable," as the Holy Father has said, "to those who are separated from the Apostolic See."

The Holy Father adds how happy he is that there are many, among our separated brethren, who have already promised to help toward the success of this important gathering. It is his fervent wish "that it should produce for the Christian family in our time that which we know to have existed in Jerusalem after the Ascension of Christ into heaven, when the new-born Church, in perfect harmony of spirit, gathered about Peter, shepherd of the sheep and of the lambs, and prayed with him."

In this atmosphere of ardent prayer, further stressed by the Unity Octave, let us reflect together on what the Council can accomplish in the present situation to promote the unity of all men who, by their baptism, are joined to Christ.

It is particularly important and necessary that Catholics not be absent from the Council. They can be present in the persons of their bishops, as the Assembly of cardinals and archbishops so strongly recommended recently in a doctrinal note on the Council: "The bishops are present at the Council . . . not as simple delegates or representatives of the Pope, but as heads of their particular church. . . . That is why, through us, your Bishops, all of you—priests, religious of our diocese, and laity—will be present at the Council."

Unity has today become the great hope, not only on a national and international level, but also on the universal plane, and hence on a religious plane as well. In fact it is on this last level that the divisions of humanity are most profound and most serious in their consequences.

An English translation of an address delivered by Augustine Cardinal Bea, S.J., in Paris, January 23, 1962. Reprinted with permission of the Paulist Press, New York, N.Y. This English translation of Cardinal Bea's address together with an English translation of an address ("The Ecumenical Council and Contemporary Thought") delivered by Joseph Cardinal Frings in Genoa, November 20, 1961 is published as a pamphlet by the Paulist Press, 180 Varick St., New York 14, N.Y., under the title: THE SECOND VATICAN COUNCIL *(25c.).*

Now it is no longer a question, merely, of unity in one country or in one nation, but of the unity of *all* Christians.

The number of Christians today has risen to about 900 million, of whom 500 million (52%) belong to the Roman Catholic Church, while the other 400 milion are composed of several independent groups called "denominations."

The fact that, since the recent assembly at New Delhi, the World Council of Churches includes 198 different religious denominations—with a goodly number of groups still outside—illustrates clearly the sad state of the unity of those who have been baptized in Christ. And yet, is it not the wish of the Church's divine Founder that there be *"one* fold and *one* shepherd"* (John 10, 16)? It is for this unity that He prayed on the eve of His passion: "I pray . . . for those also who through their word [that of the Apostles] are to believe in Me, that all may be one, even as Thou, Father, in Me and I in Thee" (John 17, 20f.).

The desire for the unity of all Christians has never been as strong as in our day. The ecumenical movement is the clearest expression of this, and the second Vatican Council proclaimed by Pope John XXIII sets out to answer this need. A non-Catholic author puts it this way: "The [Council] gives a providential impetus to the ecumenical movement. Its [proclamation] has raised great hopes among the Protestant laity throughout the world."

This fact suggests a double question: *What will be the nature of the coming Council? What will it do for unity?*

I. The Nature of the Coming Council

The lively interest aroused throughout the world by the mere proclamation of the Council is so remarkable that the Holy Father himself has said: "This respectful attention even outside the Catholic Church . . . consoles us, and gives us a foretaste of the joy of the unity of all those who believe in Christ."

The significance of this interest strikes us especially when we recall with what coldness—not to say hostility—the proclamation of the first Vatican Council was received by non-Catholics. The very thought of participating in the Council was then stiffly dismissed, and the invitations were interpreted as interference by Rome in the internal affairs of other Churches.

In our time, on the contrary, the Central Committee of the World Council of Churches declared as far back as 1959, on the day after the announcement of the Ecumenical Council: "The leaders in the ecumenical movement cannot remain indifferent in the face of this great event [the Council] which will, of necessity, have a repercussion on the relations of the Churches with one another."

At the recent reunion at New Delhi the Secretary-General of the World Council, Dr. Visser 't Hooft, quoted—not without sharing the author's conviction—these words of Professor Schlink of Heidelberg: "Undoubtedly, it will be of great importance for Christianity and for the world that the two assemblies (*i.e.*, the Vatican Council and the New Delhi Assembly) not be opposed in their decisions or seek special advantage, but that they should desire—and be seen to desire—only to serve the Lord Jesus Christ."

In the face of these favorable reactions we may well ask ourselves: *Why has the Council aroused universal esteem and interest?*

Esteem and Interest for the Council

It is not enough to answer simply that interest is due to the fact that many at first regarded the Council as a "Council of Union." It is true that the name "ecumenical council" could create this false impression. The word "ecumenical" signifies, in modern terminology, "that which is common to all Christian Churches." This could make one deduce, from the Pope's words, that he intended to invite all the Christian sects to the Council, in much the manner of the General Assembly of the World Council of Churches.

But such was not the meaning of the words of the Holy Father. The word "ecumenical" is a very old term in Canon Law and means nothing other than the "catholicity" or "universality" of the Church. In this, of course, the communion of the individual Churches with the See of Peter is implied.

An ecumenical council is, then, a council to which are invited the bishops of the entire world in communion with the Pope. The Pope could doubtless have called a "Council of Union," like those of Lyons (1274) and Florence (1439). But it is precisely those two Councils which incite us to prudence. Although they came together to re-establish unity with representatives of the schismatic Eastern Churches, unity was not effected because of the spiritual unpreparedness of the clergy and the faithful.

Misunderstanding about the Nature of the Council

This misunderstanding concerning the nature of the future Council was soon cleared up by the Holy Father himself. At the same time he made known and emphasized his profound desire for the realization of all his hopes in the Council.

Scarcely two months after the Pope proclaimed the Council he began to stress that it should offer an impressive spectacle of unity and concord within the Church. It could, in this way, serve as an invitation to those outside the jurisdiction of the Apostolic See to return to the fold confided by Christ to Peter. His Holiness repeated this thought in the first Encyclical when he mentioned that this Council should be a gentle bid "to seek and to effect that unity which Jesus Christ so earnestly implored from His heavenly Father."

Pope John XXIII constantly returns to this thought, repeating it on every possible occasion. The Secretariat for the Promotion of Christian Unity, set up at the same time as the preparatory Commissions for the Council, manifests the wholehearted interest of the Pontiff in the question of unity. His Holiness has said, in plain terms, that this Secretariat must "show our love and benevolence for those who also bear the name of Christian . . . in order that they, too, may follow the work of the Council, and thus more easily find the way that leads to that unity" willed by Christ.

Non-Catholic Impressions of the Council

We can easily imagine the *profound impression* this attitude of the Holy Father makes on those who ardently wish for unity. At a press conference held before his nomination, the new Anglican Archbishop of Canterbury, Dr. Ramsey, said: "The present Pope has, it seems to me, a great good Christian will and love. And where there is love the results are incalculable."

Orthodox prelates, too, have rendered homage to the Holy Father, one of whom, Monsignor Cassien, Rector of the Institut Saint-Serge in Paris, said: "His Holiness Pope John XXIII has seen what the others have not seen. . . . He has seen Christian unity and the supreme effort which is demanded of our faith on the road that leads to it."

One could cite a large number of similar statements, all of which show, as one Protestant author has pointed out, that the separated brethren "also expect something from the Council—for the good of all Christianity, for those of us who are divided into numerous sects, and for the common witness that we must bear before the world."

From all these considerations the following question arises: *What can the Council do to promote unity?*

2. What Can the Council Do to Promote Unity?

To this question I would answer in the words of St. Paul: "Rather are we to practice the truth in love, and so grow, in all things, in Him who is the Head, Christ" (Eph. 4, 15). Truth and charity are inseparable in this task. Truth without charity becomes intolerant and repulsive; charity without truth is blind and cannot last. The Council, too, will have to bind truth and charity together.

The Basic Dogmas of the Catholic Church

Truth must take first place. M. Lilje, Lutheran bishop of the province of Hanover, remarked—and rightly—that it would be "unthinkable for a Council to raise doubts concerning the basic dogmas of the Catholic Church."

The Lutheran bishop very clearly indicates the limitation of every Council. He does so more clearly than the Union of Protestants of the Low Countries when it asked the Netherlands episcopate recently to request the Vatican to abolish the Catholic doctrines of justification and transubstantiation. According to Protestant theologians, the latter have no literal foundation in Sacred Scripture.

It is evident that there can be no question of seeking a *compromise* touching on dogma—that is to say, on doctrine revealed by God. We would bring to the idea of unity a misguided kind of love if we sought to give non-Catholics any hope that recognition of "fundamental dogmas" is all that will be demanded of them ... or that they need not accept the decrees of the Council of Trent. Nor are we ready to re-examine the Primacy or the Infallibility of the Pope. What the Catholic Church has at one time declared to be an article of faith she has not defined arbitrarily, but rather under the inspiration of the Holy Spirit, according to the promises of Christ, "that He might guide it toward the whole truth."

Our Lord gave this spirit of truth to His Church, that she might keep and explain revealed truth rather than effect the least change in them. The Apostles were aware of the urgency of this task. With uncompromising clarity St. Paul said to the Galatians: "But even if we or an angel from heaven should preach a Gospel to you other than that which we have preached to you, let him be anathema!" (Gal. 1. 8). The Apostles and their successors possess no sovereign power over the trust which has been confided to them. They are only "administrators and dispensers of it" (1 Cor. 4. 1).

Their duty is to watch faithfully, that nothing be altered or lost. All the Councils have been conscious of this, and have never decreed *new* articles of faith nor revised the old. Their role has ever been to establish —with the assistance of the Holy Spirit and guided by Scripture and Tradition—the truth as revealed by God.

All this applies equally to the second Vatican Council. It will not consent, through a misguided irenicism, to diminish or water down the truths of the faith. Moreover, non-Catholics whose vision is clear and whose judgment is right, will not expect any such thing. The Secretary-General of the World Lutheran Association recognized this fact in an interview: "Actual Church unity has a chance of being achieved only if we place ourselves absolutely on the terrain of truth. All other means of aspiring to unity will only bring about a fictional unity."

Clarifying Misunderstandings of Catholic Doctrine

Besides, without sacrificing anything of revealed truth, the Council can efficaciously *help in recognizing the whole truth more clearly*. Those who are acquainted with the situation know to what extent false conceptions of Catholic doctrine and practice block the road to unity. Some of these misunderstandings go back to the early period of the Reformation. Others arise from differences in the theological terminology, or derive from the influence exercised on Protestant theology by various philosophical trends during the last few centuries.

It is a fact that philosophical systems not only express the mentality of the age, but also exercise a more or less powerful influence on the minds of men. Inevitably, they have an effect, too, on theological language ... the more so when this theology is less tied to tradition and less controlled by doctrinal authority. We can therefore easily see that the various modern philosophical systems have exercised considerable influence on religious thought and on Protestant theological language. Thus non-Catholics often find it very difficult to grasp Catholic doctrine expressed in the traditional language of the Church.

It will be necessary, therefore, as the Holy Father has told us, "to return to the pure sources of revelation and tradition, and to restore to its original value and splendor the substance of Christian thought and life, of which the Church has been the repository and teacher for centuries."

To the difficulties of theological terminology another and even more important element must be added. Many of the theological assertions made in the formulation of defined, unchanging doctrine must be examined in the light of the historical circumstances in which they were written. Sometimes they present only a *certain aspect of the doctrine,* instead of giving all the abundance and profundity of available truth. In his encyclical *Humani Generis,* Pius XII stated that "the two sources of the doctrine revealed by God (Scripture and Tradition) contain treasures of truth so great and so numerous that they will never be fully exhausted."

That is why we shall have to search once more in this treasury of revealed truth for those elements which are of the greatest importance to non-Catholics in this moment. Thus, in clarifying certain matters that are particularly pertinent to our time, the Council will not only dispel a large number of misunderstandings touching on Catholic doctrine, but also bring out again, from the richness and depths of the truths of the faith, those truths that are of special concern today.

The present age is *particularly favorable* to this venture. The modern scientific movement is characterized by a remarkable revival of interest in history and the social structure of life. We are now examining the origin and historical development of ideas. We are studying the environment in which those ideas were born, and their survival, along with such influences as they have undergone.

Individualism—long the predominant influence in the intellectual world, an influence which extended its undesirable effects to the field of theological studies—is now giving way to this historical and sociological method. Religious thought, like theological research, is once again finding its place in the stream of tradition.

This modern method is particularly rich in results when applied to *the study of Sacred Scripture.* Take, for example, a well-known Protestant theologian of the University of Zurich and his review of Kittel's *Theological Dictionary of the New Testament.* He declares that in the *Dictionary* "it is the New Testament itself that speaks, and not the classical exegetical tradition of any single confession...." The reviewer notes further: "In the light of the results of the *Theological Dictionary* certain classical theological doctrines of our forefathers regarding the faith reveal themselves as biblical only in a very limited sense." As an example, the doctrines of original sin and predestination are mentioned; and the reviewer notes that Luther's conception of justification by faith alone cannot—without qualification—be identified with that of St. Paul.

Then, too, there is the question of the *definition of unity.* In the past a certain number of Protestant theologians opposed the idea of a visible unity. The General Assembly at New Delhi has made a proposal as a result of studies jointly undertaken by different denominations. It suggests that the unity of the Church "is made manifest by the fact that all those who have been baptized in Jesus Christ, and who acknowledge Him as Lord and Savior, are led by the Holy Spirit to form one community —to confess the same apostolic faith—to preach the same Gospel—to share the same bread—and to unite together in common prayer ... being in communion with the whole community of Christians in all times and places."

Although this description of unity may not yet be completely identical with the view held by Catholics, it nevertheless indicates the results obtained by a deeper study of Sacred Scripture and of Christian tradition.

In one of the conferences organized by the *Christian Humanities* of Strasbourg in November, 1961, its president Marc Boegner, speaking on the subject of Mary and Peter, declared that he could not accept the Marian "nihilism" of Protestants. On the question of Peter he added that one should have the loyalty to study the problem and to follow the consequences through to the end.

From this it becomes evident that a more perfect and thorough method of scientific research in theology can considerably reduce the traditional differences in the field of doctrine. The Council—and, after it, the scientific work of theologians—will be able to make various Catholic articles of faith more acceptable to Protestants by indicating their origin in Sacred Scripture.

In this way many doubts and obscurities can be discarded. Dr. Ramsey, Archbishop of Canterbury, rightly affirmed at New Delhi: "Among Roman Catholics, Lutherans, Orthodox, the Reformed Churches, and the Anglicans one may observe interest in the Bible, the Fathers and the liturgy, a circumstance which opens up new avenues of thought and new possibilities in the field of teaching. It brings new plans for discussion and association into the light."

Doctrine on the Nature of the Church

This last remark is of particular interest with regard to *doctrine about the Church*. Indeed it is the most serious point of difference separating Catholics, Protestants and, in part, the Orthodox. Moreover, many Protestants have themselves become aware that what matters most is precisely this getting to know the true doctrine regarding the Church of Christ. They even speak of a "re-discovery" of the Church. "In reality," says a contemporary Swiss Protestant theologian, "it is precisely the question of the Church that Protestant research has not yet been able to solve."

The Council may well be able to throw new light on the various differences in the field. The question of the nature of the Church was posed as far back as the Council of Trent. But neither at that Council nor at the first Vatican Council was this fundamental matter dealt with in a way sufficiently profound and thorough. It will be the task of this coming Council to complete a work that has been considerably facilitated in our day by important research conducted by qualified theologians. Above all, it will be facilitated by the penetrating exposition of doctrine on the Church offered us by Pope Pius XII in his Encyclical on the Mystical Body of Christ. Certain qualified Protestant writers have admitted that this Encyclical presented an idea of the Church earlier unknown to them.

With regard to the most difficult point of all for non-Catholics—the question of the *primacy* of Peter—Pope John XXIII has, in his turn, created a much more favorable climate of opinion by demonstrating—through his own example of charity, good will, and humility—that the Roman Church understands and practices this primacy—as Msgr. Dumont has observed—not from a desire to dominate but as a service, a "diaconia."

The mere fact of the convocation of an Ecumenical Council shows that the Sovereign Pontiff in no way discounts the collaboration of the bishops in the government of the Church. The doctrine proclaiming the Church to be the "Mystical Body of Christ," like the co-operation between Pontiff and bishops, and also that attitude of humble service, should serve to clarify a mass of points once baffling to non-Catholics. Many of these difficulties will hereafter be seen to be unfolded.

We cannot go deeper into these matters at this time. Moreover, an assembly of French cardinals and bishops has recently issued a very clear doctrinal statement on this question for the instruction of the faithful. We would simply like to emphasize that the Council will be able to clarify many points regarding the nature of the Church.

Ecumenical Task of the Church

Let us turn to another question: the *ecumenical task* of the Church. In our day we often refer to our "separated brethren." This is not only a courteous designation, but also an expression of a profound Christian truth. All those who have been validly baptized in Christ—even outside the Catholic Church—are organically bound to Christ through baptism. They have been bound to His Mystical Body. "In spite of our ecclesiastical, theological, or human differences all are brothers, because we all know that we depend solely on the grace of our Lord Jesus Christ." (These are the words of Philippe Maury, Secretary-General of the World Federation of Christian Students at the *Pax Romana* congress held last August in Fribourg, Switzerland.)

We should, then, aspire, pray, and work to the end that all those who are baptized should participate in all the gifts of truth and grace that derive from our divine Head, Christ. The distribution of these gifts has been entrusted to the Church by Christ Himself. Unfortunately, there are many—too many—who still remain outside the Church and the vivifying current of graces that flow from her.

Admittedly, these persons, by virtue of their baptism, possess a union of grace with Christ. This union allows them an authentic religious life, such as we admire in many of our separated brothers. It helps them to develop their life of faith and gives them the strength to overcome difficulties met upon the way. But how many other graces do they fail to receive? Those, for instance, that would reach them through the sacraments of the Church. . . . That is why the Church feels obligated, not only as a result of our Lord's explicit command, but also as a sacred duty of charity, to help them find the way that leads to this fullness of grace.

This desire of the Church does not spring from any form of "imperialism," or from a need "to dominate," or from "totalitarianism," or from a "question of prestige." It arises from a true and authentic maternal love. The Church is convinced—and is under obligation to be convinced—that Christ has entrusted her with the salvation of all those who are validly baptized. They are, by this very fact, "children" of the Church, even as the Holy Father called them in the important Apostolic Constitution, *Humanae Salutis,* of December 25, 1961.

This is the origin of the motherly anxiety that the Church feels for all men. It is understandable that others do not share our faith. But this cannot, indeed must not, in any way be considered a reason for doubting the *sincerity* of the Catholic Church. Neither should it suggest different motives behind her attitude, much less motives that would do her little credit, when she is seen to promote "unity" and "reunion."

141

Who Is Responsible for the Separation?

In this connection it is frequently said that the Church bears *responsibility for the separation,* and thus should frankly and contritely acknowledge her fault. Certainly it is with great sorrow, as the Holy Father has emphasized, that we recall the fact that these divisions are the result of self-love and pride, and of a refusal to bear in mind the teaching of our Lord: "Learn from Me, for I am meek and humble of heart." Note, however, that it is not a question of the Church as a whole but of certain *members* of the Church—of men who in past centuries such as the 11th and 16th—guided or governed the Church, whether a part or the whole of it, or who simply belonged to the Church.

We must be careful, moreover, not to confuse dogmatic with moral responsibility. The decrees drawn up by the Council of Trent show clearly that the Church was in need of reform in the practical domain of customs and morals. But on the dogmatic or doctrinal level, she was always guided by the Holy Spirit and was never led astray; she could not be.

Besides, have we the right today to judge those who lived in distant ages? It is God alone who can judge in this. The generations that have followed the break simply cannot comprehend the unbelievable tangle of authentic religious aspirations, human passions, and base personal or political interests which then existed. It is clearly impossible to weigh the degree of blame borne by one person or another. Let us leave the past in peace, and busy ourselves, rather, with winning back what has been lost: *the unity of all Christians, of all baptized.*

The "Unity" Desired by Christ

At this point, however, another problem arises. In the view of one Protestant theologian, "a holy Church of Christ according to the Gospel," is nothing other than "the community of Christians who wish to live a life of faith and grace—the grace of Christ—and who travel the way that will lead them to their eternal goal." This unity, he claims, is not, by its very nature, "organized." The "true Church of Christ may even now be found within all our Churches, in spite of the differences of doctrine and faith."

We, too, have clearly and strongly asserted this fact of the interior unity of all the baptized. But is this all? Was it the will of the divine Founder of the Church to create only an invisible unity? This is a question that cannot be decided with simple reference to "the idea that the Church of Rome has within herself" the *"Selbstverständnis"* or self-evidence of the Church. The question must be solved with the aid of the Gospels and the writings of the Apostles—and, indeed, from the Old Testament prophecies regarding the future Kingdom of God.

In order to decide what this "unity" is that was desired by Christ, we cannot rely merely on our human competence. It would be more fitting to submit ourselves, with all humility and obedience, to an impartial, objective, methodically exact interpretation of Sacred Scriptures, revealed to us as the express will of the divine Founder of the Church. There, again, the Council, guided by the Holy Spirit, the Spirit of the Mystical Body of Christ, will have to utter the decisive word. In this work of fraternal research conducted in a spirit of charity and in serious discussion, the science of theology will undertake to lay hold of and present the scriptural foundation of Catholic doctrine on the true unity of the Church.

We were happy to note that at New Delhi the "Faith and Constitution" committee asked that "the possibility of meetings with the Roman Catholics should be specially borne in mind," and that "the member Churches and local councils should take every measure that they might consider desirable in this field." Friendly meetings between Catholic and non-Catholic theologians will serve to underline the truth of the words spoken some days ago by a well-known personality of the Reformed Church in France: "However serious may be the issues that divide us, what unites us is much greater" (cf. *La Croix*, 17–5–1962, p. 4).

This short survey may serve to highlight the importance of the Council in connection with teachings on the nature of the Church and on unity.

Naturally, there are numerous other points of doctrine that the Council will serve to clarify. We may mention, for instance, the question of the place of the layman in the Church, (a special preparatory Commission has been set up to study this matter); the possibility of communicating under both species and the incorporation of the ancient hierarchies of the Oriental Churches into the total structure of the Church. There are also many questions in which the Council will bear in mind the "ecumenical" situation, while making decisions and offering solutions to the varied and important problems regarding non-Catholics.

Certainly, there is no lack of suggestions and proposals submitted to the Council! A great number of these reach our Secretariat for the Promotion of Christian Unity. There they are examined in the course of serious study and discussion, after which the results are sent on to the respective Commissions of the Council.

Besides the field of dogma there are vast areas pertaining to *canon law, public worship, and private religious practice.* In these matters, the nature of which does not ordinarily depend on an unchangeable command of God, the divine Founder of the Church has allowed a much greater degree of freedom. As the liturgy, religious practice, and the history of canon law show, the Church has always, and to a great extent, taken into account the needs of the times, the different customs of peoples, and the demands of pastoral work.

Pope John XXIII himself has already indicated that the Council intends to follow this same line of conduct. In his discourse of January 25, 1959, the Holy Father mentioned, among the tasks to be undertaken by the Council, that of "the reform of canon law so ardently desired and awaited." The Cardinal-Secretary of the Holy Office recently stated, in a public discourse, in what spirit this reform and other similar ones of a practical nature should be undertaken: "Once truth is acknowledged, truth about which the Church cannot compromise, all those who draw near will find in her a mother disposed to make every possible concession regarding the liturgy and various customs and disciplinary measures at the human level."

From this summary it seems clear that the bodies responsible for the preparation of the Council are fully informed as to the aspirations and proposals regarding unity. There is already a vast amount of material available on the question of unity in 15 folio volumes containing the reports of bishops from all over the world, of theological faculties and universities and other institutions. These volumes are at the disposal of each member and consultant of the Preparatory Commissions.

Add to this the fact that the Commissions, and especially the Central Commission, are composed of specialists from many different nations. It would seem unnecessary to emphasize the quantity and value of data regarding different religious situations, experiences, and other varied information, which converges—for the benefit of the Council—on these international bodies from many parts of the globe.

In addition to publications, in various languages, about the Council, a vast amount of correspondence arrives from different nations. Letters addressed to the heads or the members of the Commissions make every possible kind of proposal. We may be sure that everything which is at all essential is to be found in these documents. We would like to point out, moreover, that many of the letters come from lay persons interested in the life of the Church; these make a precious contribution to the preparation of the Council. We can say, without hesitation, that in all the 2,000 years of the history of the Church, no Council has been prepared as thoroughly as this one.

The Ecumenical Movement

There is yet another area in which the Council will be able to perform some useful work; that is, in promoting the *ecumenical movement*.

We have already spoken of the theological basis underlying the work of Catholics with regard to the union of Christians. That the idea of unity constitutes such a potent force in our times is, without doubt, a most special grace offered by the Holy Spirit. Yet this grace obliges us, too, as Catholics, to collaborate with all our strength in the work of the re-establishment of the unity of all Christians—to strive to overcome courageously any prejudices that may, perhaps, linger on—and to forget the inherited wounds and susceptibilities of the past.

Here, too, the Council will be able to emphasize, above all, that the Catholic has the highest duty to take an interest in the welfare of his separated brothers and, consequently, to pray, make sacrifices and work for the unity of all those baptized in Christ.

Could we not say that the contribution toward unity of Christians today is still too individual and divided? It is true that much has already been done. One need only to think of the Unity Octave in which we are taking part these days, along with so many of our separated brethren. Many theological conversations are taking place in numerous conferences, articles and publications dedicated to the question of unity.

Without any idea of centralizing or standardizing, the Council will be able to indicate the lines of conduct to be followed in these activities, and to point out what can be achieved. It will be able to make clear how, whether individually or collectively, all Christians may share in this immense task. Above all, it will be able to define the means which are at the disposal of *all* those who are "children" of the Church.

Among these means, *prayer,* beyond doubt, will hold first place, as the Holy Father has so often pointed out, and as the Ecumenical Council of Churches at New Delhi demanded in its "appeal to the heart and conscience of all member churches, that they should understand the importance of constant prayer for their Christian brothers throughout the world."

Prayer should be accompanied by *sacrifice,* by the daily offering of our sufferings, troubles and setbacks, for the over-all intention of unity, and of that *charity* which the Apostle Paul praises in his letter to the Corinthians. Of the latter the Holy Father has given a magnificent example by his own preference for "underscoring those things that unite men, and by his readiness to accompany others as far as is possible without compromising either the needs of justice or the rights of truths."

The Council will also open up possibilities of close *collaboration in areas not touching upon the faith.* It will do so in the affirmation of ideas that have to do with the natural moral law or that constitute the common heritage of all Christians, as well as by work undertaken for the good of the suffering and oppressed. Moreover, it will be able to recommend and promote the kind of serious, theological discussion desired by our separated brethren, as we have already mentioned.

Finally, it may be suggested that all seminarians should early be instructed as to the importance, the difficulties, and the methods of the movement toward unity, and should be encouraged to become its enthusiastic adherents.

Thus, though it will not be a "Council of Union," the second Vatican Council will nevertheless be able to make an important contribution toward unity, and to lay the foundation which, at God's moment, when we ourselves and our separated brothers are sufficiently prepared—will enable us to hold a true "Council of Union." This will at last make a reality of our Lord's desire that there be but "one flock and one shepherd."

Conclusions

Is the hope that we shall one day attain this end utopian—an illusion? We have demonstrated in a realistic manner that the diffculties on the way to union are still very great, and that in many ways we and non-Catholics are still far apart. It would be useless to deceive ourselves on this point. But to lose courage and to remain inactive would be as bad.

Let us join with Monsignor Cassien whom we quoted earlier: "It is God who guides history. But what is required of us—understanding and charity—is already, in our state of separation, an expression of our unity."

One thing is absolutely certain: the unity of all those who have been baptized is *the will of God*. That is why, on the eve of His Passion, the Savior 'addressed this ardent prayer to His heavenly Father: "Holy Father, keep in Thy Name those whom Thou hast given Me, that they may be one even as We are . . . that they may also be one in Us, that the world may believe that Thou has sent Me . . . I, in them, and Thou in Me; that they may be perfected in unity."

We can and must work with all our strength to fulfill this Divine Will. Let us not forget, however, what St. Paul once said on this subject to the Corinthians: "I have planted, Apollos has watered, but God has given the growth . . . for we are God's helpers."

The outcome, the progress, is God's business. But God is *all-powerful*. Let us remember the reply that Jesus gave to His disciples who, in their boldness, had come to Him with an objection: "With men this is impossible, but with God all things are possible."

Hence we go forth, full of confidence and courage, in charity, and in a spirit of prayer, sacrifice, and work, upon the way that leads to the unity of all who have been baptized in Christ; while we bear in mind the words of St. Paul: "For it is God who of His good pleasure works in you both the will and the performance."

Hans Küng

Can the Council Fail?

*E*veryone who takes on a public role in the interests of the coming Council feels time and again how great, on the one hand, are the expectations which have been awakened by the announcement of the Second Vatican Council, and how small, on the other, is the certainty that these great expectations will be fulfilled. It is easy to see how much the original interest of many Catholics and Evangelical Protestants in the Council has dwindled and how far a deep skepticism has spread even among theologians and the educated classes.

This is not just the result of a fundamental misunderstanding of the nature of an "ecumenical" Council, which is not meant to be an assembly of all the churches, but of the Roman Catholic Church. Nor is it to be explained merely by saying that, outside our own Church, too little attention is paid to this ecumenical complexion of the coming Council, which will prevent it from becoming simply "an internal Catholic concern." But it is connected very definitely with the doubt whether, in the error and confusion of the present day, the Council will take the decisive step which the need of the Church in this hour of the world's history demands. No one, inside or outside the Church, has any reservations about the good intention of the Pope, whose action, so rich in consequences, will in any case be regarded as epoch-making in Church history. Nor does anyone doubt the good will of those who are making the preparations for the Council, among whom are some outstanding men who are certainly taking the greatest pains, and by hard and selfless work doing their utmost to ensure the proper preparation of this assembly. But various facts have given much more cause to doubt whether the Council, despite all the good intentions and all the good will and all the hard work, will attain its major objectives.

In this context, the following points are often brought forward for serious consideration: the Roman Diocesan Synod, which left no room

Father Hans Küng is the author of The Council, Reform and Reunion *(Sheed and Ward), a book which should be read in conjunction with this issue. Professor of Theology at the University of Tübingen, he is also famous for his study of the notion of justification in Karl Barth and the Council of Trent* (Rechtfertigung: Die Lehre Karl Barths und eine Katholische Besinnung *(Einsiedeln, 1957). The present article appeared in* Rheinischer Merkur *(Oct. 28, 1961); an except was translated in the Irish monthly,* The Furrow, *and was reprinted in* The Commonweal.

for free discussion and made no energetic reforms; then, in certain Roman circles (not all, of course) the lack of ecumenical outlook, Catholic openness and practical readiness for an exchange of views; the way reunion as the ultimately determining goal of the Council is pushed into the background at Vatican press conferences; the unusually high average age of the Cardinals of the Curia; the uneven representation of territorial bishoprics (for example, about 290 Italian bishops and 26 German); the rejection of a system of simultaneous translation in favor of Latin; the badly working Press Secretariat; the efforts directed by certain Roman circles against the Papal Biblical Institute and various well-known Catholic exegetes, and so on. One can not only hear these things said time and again in private conversations and discussions, but can also read them in the press.

What is the believing Christian to think in the face of this skepticism? In particular, what is the parish priest, professor, journalist, or lecturer to do when he must express himself responsibly on the question of the Council (and it would be a good thing if more of it were done)?

Two Attitudes

The first of two possible attitudes is the way of facile apologetic: you deal with difficulties point by point, making distinctions in each with a "Quite true, of course—but you see." While you are at it, you repeat some point which no one doubts is correct, but happens to be irrelevant, and come finally to the soothing conclusion that things are not really so depressing after all. Indeed, the really depressing people are those who presented things in such a bad light. What does this approach accomplish? It helps to train good "partyline" Catholics who will not read this article because they prefer to believe that everything in the Church is necessarily for the best. But men who think of the needs of the age and study the Church with watchful eyes, find this attitude at best a type of well-meaning apologetic, most unhelpful at the present moment, since it merely glosses over real difficulties. Disappointed by this response, they are losing hope that among our Church leaders the problems are seen for what they are; in their minds they write off the coming Council.

These theologians, who seem committed to such cut-rate apologetics, give the impression that they have learned nothing since the First Vatican Council, and seem to believe that in spite of the enormous needs of the world and of the Christian people, nothing has changed. In such circumstances the Council for reunion will not result in much more than fine words and invitations. In this way Catholic apologetics causes either a comfortable or a defeatist inactivity.

The second approach is that of honest and sincere reflection: in the interest of the Church and of the Council black is here called black, grey grey, and white white, and no attempt is made (at least not in a lecture or article) to put a neat little patch over every difficulty—which in any case does not prove to be a real repair. In this approach the difficulties are acknowledged to be real ones, but the accent is laid more on the positive aspects of the Council's approach to problems:

1. The ecumenical outlook of the present Pope, which gives comfort and strength to so many Christians, and his great program for the Council: "Through the renewal of the Catholic Church to reunion of separated Christians!"

2. The positive factors in the preparations for the Council: the changed ecumenical climate in the Universal Church through the initiative of the Pope; the setting up of the Roman "Secretariat for the Promotion of Christian Unity" under the outstanding leadership of Cardinal Bea; the basic linking of reunion with the self-reform of our own Church, and so on.

3. The positive possibilities of realizing the Council's program, both in principle and practice.

It is in this way that skepticism and defeatism can be countered and, while retaining a firm realism, hope and courage can be strengthened. Such intellectual honesty is a call to action in the service of the Council's aims.

What the Church of today needs is, first of all, honesty—honesty in the appraisal, free of all illusion, of the situation of our own Church and of the others; and in the second place, courage—courage to speak out, *opportune importune,* concerning what .the situation demands in the light of the Gospel of Jesus Christ, even at the great risk of making oneself unpopular; and finally, a readiness for action—a readiness for unceasing work in the place to which the Lord God has assigned one, for the realization of the goal of the Council.

Convocation by God and Convocation by Man

We must now pose a key question: can the Council result in a failure in regard to its essential aims? Of course, it is easy enough to say that the mere calling of an Ecumenical Council does not automatically assure its essential success. A Council can be called, and never meet. A pope might annul it, or refuse to approve of specific conclusions at which the assembly arrived. But we must look a little more deeply into our question.

We may state that in principle an Ecumenical Council can deviate from its essential ends because of various human or too-human factors. Of course, there is no Council that does not have some happy consequences, direct or indirect, obvious or hidden. For those who love God, everything seems ultimately to work for the good. But as much (or little) could be said of any assembly. A Council may very well determine a series of happy consequences, and nevertheless, taken as a whole, meet a fundamental setback as regards its essential purposes. We believe strongly in the help of the Holy Spirit which has been promised to the Church, and hence to the Council as well. But the help of the Holy Spirit does not necessarily preserve the Council from failure. At this level, we must distinguish carefully between that Ecumenical Council *directly convoked by God*—which is the Church, and the Ecumenical Council *convoked by men*. The latter is the most representative expression of the Church, but it remains, nevertheless, only an expression. God's convocation gives assurance at the outset of the graces necessary in order that the Council which is the Church should avoid any overall failure. The convocation by men does not similarly give advance assurance of authentic success.

The Church does not fail, even if a Council called by her were to fail. As a single event in the unfolding of the history of the Church, the Council may very well not respond in a useful way to the demands of the hour. The *particular* help of the Spirit is essentially negative; it protects from all error. It is not positive, and in any case it does not act miraculously to give assurance of a complete success in spite of the incapacities and incompetence of men. The consequence of this *essentially human* character of the Ecumenical Council called by men is that, in contrast to the Council called by God, it can show itself to be incapable of realizing its major objectives. A Council can be assembled, magnificent ceremonies can take place, there may be proclamations and excommunications, but the necessities of the age, and the real needs of the Church for that age, may not have been met.

To see that this is not a pure hypothesis, we need only to study the history of the Fifth Lateran Council (1512–1517). "In spite of all hesitations," Jedin writes, "in spite of all the significant considerations that have been raised against this council, it was saluted with enthusiasm as the dawn of a new and better day, as the beginning of the reform of the Church."[1] The inaugural discourse of the general of the Augustianians, Egidius of Viterbo, presented the reform of the Church as the principal task of the Council. Two Venetians who had just entered the Camaldians, Tommaso Giustiniani and Vincenzo Quirini, presented a vast plan of reform, "the most complete and radical that had ever been presented in the era of the councils."[2] The Ecumenical Council was then convoked, and its essential objectives were clearly defined. They condemned Averroïsm, they spoke a great deal about reforms, but it all ended in failure. "We may say without exaggeration," Jedin continues, "that the plan for reform submitted by the two Camaldian fathers contained what was needed to give a direction to the Church for more than a century. The Council of Trent, the liturgical reforms of Pius V, the Sixtine Bible, the foundation of the Congregation of Propaganda, were all

---

1 H. Jedin, *Geschichte des Konzils von Trent*, Freiburg-B., 1951, vol. 1, p. 90.
2 *Op. cit.*, p. 103.

clearly indicated in it. But the pope for whom they wrote and the council which assembled before their eyes were incapable of following these well-founded and truly prophetic views. They deceived the hopes that were placed in them."[3] This failure of an Ecumenical Council, which lasted for years, constituted a real catastrophe for the Church: six months later Luther's reform broke out.

Fruitless Doctrinal Definitions?

We may certainly include doctrinal definitions among the results of a Council. But the example of the Fifth Lateran Council shows us that the promulgation of infallible doctrinal definitions does not mean that, taken as a whole, the Council has realized the objectives that were assigned to it. There are theologians, of course, who cannot think of failure in this connection, except in the sense that a certain number of men might noisily reject the truth that the Church had just proclaimed. Their lapidary formula satisfies them: "Truth knows no failures."

The question that is worth considering, however, is a different one: is it enough that a Council define certain doctrinal points for it to be considered a real success? Surely we all agree that there has been no definition which has not had happy consequences, directly or indirectly, obviously or secretly. But a definition, although perfectly exact in itself, does not guarantee that a Council has attained its essential purposes, if we are to take an over-all view of things. A definition can be true without corresponding to the needs of the time. It can overlook the real needs of the age and of the Church. It was not enough for the Fifth Lateran Council to define the intellectual soul as the substantial form of the body for one to be able to claim that it had attained its true purpose.

Too many theologians consider only the number of doctrinal definitions. On this subject various rumors have been spread, and we must hope that the preparatory theological commission of the Second Vatican Council will have a clearer view of things. Besides, the history of this commission at the First Vatican Council is enlightening: it busied itself with a great number of possible definitions, but various factors, not simply the lack of time, caused very few proposals to be retained, and then only after having been radically amended. In any case, the various statements of Pope John show that he is only secondarily concerned with declarations, excommunications, anathemas or new dogmas.

It will, perhaps, be said that "The Church cannot be silent, when the situation and truth demand that she speak out loud and clear." But it may be replied that it would be a great fault if the Church were to speak when the situation and truth call for her to be quiet and avoid definitions. Essentially, it would be a matter of deciding on questions

---

[3] *Op. cit.*, p. 104.

which are still debated among Catholic theologians. The directives of Pius IV at the Council of Trent remain up to date: he demanded that in the examination of important dogmatic questions, definitions should be attempted only when the *unanimous agreement* of the Fathers had been obtained. This clause was not easy to realize. According to the great Catholic tradition, it is necessary to be dogmatic only when the danger of heresy is clear. It is not without reason that John XXIII recalled that golden rule for doctrinal controversy among Catholics: *In necessariis unitas, in dubiis libertas, in omnibus caritas.*

Should the occasion arise, the Council should combat the errors of an age. This affirmation scarcely needs to be backed dogmatically, in these times when the Magisterium takes positions on innumerable occasions in relation to the errors of the day. Nevertheless, the task of a Council is not the same as that of theology, and it should not try to replace it. We may note, first of all, that it would be impossible to expect a decision on all questions in dispute from more than 2000 bishops who cannot remain away from their dioceses indefinitely. But it may happen that, just as at the First Vatican Council, this difficulty may not be taken into account.

Take, for example, the question of episcopacy. A theologian whose formation was in terms of 19th-century neo-scholasticism will say that it is enough to assemble the various elements of current theological thinking in order to present a clear and tidy Catholic doctrine. But what was sufficient in 1870 is no longer so today. Just compare the often simplistic presentations with which people were satisfied then with recent work in this area. The older studies remained almost exclusively on the level of canon law, and sometimes relied on dubious historical data. In the work of Karl Rahner and Joseph Ratzinger[4] (as well as several French scholars), however, we attain a more truly theological level without neglecting canonical evidence. They carefully recognize the various aspects of this very complex problem, without neglecting any of its difficulties, and they examine meticulously the exegetical, historical, theological and canonical aspects of the various questions raised. They are not satisfied with repeating general and vague formulas, they are seeking a deeper understanding and arrive at many elements of a solution, both at the theoretical and the practical level.

On this point, then, as on so many others which will be examined at the Council, it is imperative that we go beyond the too exclusively canonical conceptions of the 19th century in order to attain to the level of authentic theology. Progress that has been made in various areas of theological research, particularly in the domain of exegesis, the history of dogma, the history of the Church, or the history of law, must be taken into account.

It is especially important to observe the repercussions of a doctrinal

---

[4] *'Episkopat und Primat*, Quaestiones disputatae 11, Freiburg-Basel-Wien, 1961.

definition at the level of ecumenical activities. According to the pope's intention, the Council is essentially to aim at a renewal of the Church for the purpose of reunion. Everything which might compromise this aim should be put aside. Useless definitions which would risk accentuating and deepening divisions would tend by that very fact to make the Council deviate from its major end. From this point of view, it is obvious that the definition, for example, of a Marian dogma, would be a disservice to the cause of reunion. It must be said in all clarity: it is not a question of opportunism, but a matter of genuine moral responsibility. A confession must not give special emphasis to what is particular to it unless there is an over-riding necessity; otherwise it would be forgetting its share of responsibility for divisions, and its duty to do everything possible to reduce obstacles. St. Paul demanded that everything be avoided that might constitute a stumbling block for his feeble brethren and their faith in Christ. Are we to forget this and neglect the requirements of this fraternal charity that Our Lord has so strongly prescribed?[5]

Reforms without Results?

We have seen that a Council can prove incapable of realizing its historical objectives. If, in the domain of doctrinal definitions, a theologian may prefer not to give emphasis to this necessary but delicate truth, he can scarcely avoid it when he considers ecclesiastical reforms. When we speak of a setback in regard to a Council, we think, first of all, of reforms which were avoided or neglected. Of course, disciplinary decisions and new laws or reforms do not proceed in opposition to revelation, but that does not mean that they are a valid response to the needs of our time and the deepest needs of the Church. The fact is clear: when a Council assembles, as the coming one will, with a reform in view, it can fail in terms of its major purpose.

There will be frank rejoicing if the reforms envisaged for the future Council are crowned with success, and if it proves to be more fortunate than the First Vatican Council. We know of the tremendous number of suggestions in regard to diverse reforms that were then collected; 300 in-folio columns were needed to record them; there were 46 plans in regard to discipline, four of which were discussed, with none finally approved! Interminable discussions dragged on from January 8th to February 22, 1870, and were resumed in May, after a reshuffling of plans. As for the preparatory reports on the religious orders, the Eastern Churches and the missions, there was no opportunity to discuss them. In some degree, lack of time explains this failure. But there are also other reasons, especially the two following:

1) The preparatory work was done with great zeal, but in too unilat-

---

5 O. Karrer, *Spiritualität und Dogma in ökumenischer Fragestellung, in Kirche und Überlieferung,* Festschrift für R. Geiselmann. Freiburg-Basel-Wien.

eral a manner, not taking sufficiently into account the areas and different currents of opinion with respect to which the bishops were called upon to pronounce.

2) Instead of examining important questions in the light of the gospel, one got bogged down in details, often of quite a secondary importance, and ended in long digressions. Archbishop Darboy of Paris remarked in the midst of conciliar discussions: "We are going hither and yon in a maze of details, among the pointless and inconsistent *placita* of various schools. We discuss items of canon law with tremendous care and get lost in all kinds of childishness. Some were afraid to see the Vatican Council take on a task which exceeded the possibilities of an assembly which is far too sick. I am seized with the fear . . . [that] at all cost the Council must not show itself as inferior to the task that it has assumed in the eyes of those who make public opinion, that queen of the world."[6]

The Consequences of the Future Council

When may we consider a Council to have succeeded? And in particular, how will the future Council achieve its true end? Everyone agrees that we are living in a period of upheaval. It calls for extraordinary means. It is not enough "to hold on to tradition" and to affirm that "the truth can be hard." Nor is it enough "to wage the good fight against error" and to justify decisions "to exclude from the community of the faithful, with all the consequences anticipated by law." We cannot be satisfied to ask others "to recognize the ministry of Peter perpetuated in the Church," or "to return to the Father's house," or to recall "the road to Rome." In such conditions, how could we realize the proximate end of the Council which is the renewal of the Church, or its ultimate end which is reunion?

At all costs, it is imperative that, in all the sectors of our Church, it be well understood that the Council will meet with failure only if it gets lost in details. But on what conditions will it be able really to produce something significant? All those who, in various ways, work with a genuine success in view are completely certain: success will be achieved neither by opportunistic "modernizations" nor by traditionalist patchwork. What is needed is a theological and practical reflection on the Gospel of Jesus Christ Our Lord, a reflection that is pursued in contact with current data and in terms of our time, under the influence of the Holy Spirit.

translated by G. WATSON *and* F. X. QUINN

---

[6] Butler-Lang, *Das Vatikanische Konzil*, München, 1933; p. 175 ff.